SMALL GARDEN...
BITTER WEED

George Beckford
Michael Witter

SMALL GARDEN... BITTER WEED

The Political Economy of Struggle and Change in Jamaica

George Beckford
Michael Witter

Maroon Publishing House,
Morant Bay, Jamaica.

Zed Books Ltd.
57 Caledonian Road, London N1 9BU, UK

Limited Student and Electoral Edition,
October 1980
Second (Expanded) Edition, January 1982

Small Garden . . . Bitter Weed (Second, expanded edition) was first published by Maroon Publishing House, Morant Bay P.O., St. James, Jamaica, and by Zed Press, 57 Caledonian Road, London N1 9BU in January 1982.

1st Reprint 1984
2nd Reprint 1985

Copyright © 1980 by M. Witter and G. Beckford
All rights reserved

ISBN 0 86232 003 8 Hb
ISBN 0 86232 008 9 Pb

All correspondence to:
Managing Editor
Maroon Publishing House
Morant Bay P.O., St. Thomas, JAMAICA

Cover illustration by Mervin Palmer
Printed by The Bath Press, Avon.

We record our gratitude to two sisters who volunteered typing services at critical moments. First, Carol Lindo who for days and nights typed, from dictation, the first rough draft of what was to become this book, and secondly, Christine Cummings who typed the Epilogue.

TABLE OF CONTENTS

LIST OF DIAGRAMS	xiii
LIST OF ABBREVIATIONS	xvii
PREFACE	xiv

CHAPTER

1   **PEOPLE, SOCIETIES AND CHANGE:**   1
The Study of Political Economy
    1. The Anatomy of Society
    2. The Dynamics of Social Change

2   **FROM EUROPEAN CONQUEST TO EMANCIPATION**   12
    1. Conquest of the Americas
    2. English Colonization
    3. Slave Plantation Society
    4. Emancipation: Class Struggles in Jamaica and England

3   **EUROPEAN CAPITALISM, COLONIALISM AND IMPERIALISM**   23
    1. Mercantile Capitalism
    2. Industrial Capitalism
    3. Monopoly Capitalism
    4. Capitalism, Colonialism and Imperialism

4   **EMERGENCE OF THE PEASANTRY IN THE WOMB OF IMPERIALISM:**   36
From Emancipation to 1865
    1. Birth of Capitalism in Jamaica
    2. Peasant Struggle, State Repression and the Birth of Imperialism
    3. Class Formation

CHAPTER		Page
5	EMERGENCE OF THE WORKING CLASS: From the Morant Bay Rebellion to 1938	49

    1. The Banana Trade
    2. Forms of Resistance
    3. Shockwaves from Imperialist Crisis
    4. A Hundred Years of Struggle, 1838 — 1938

| 6 | BIRTH AND GROWTH OF THE NATIONAL ECONOMY: 1938–1962 | 61 |

    1. The Political Party Struggle
    2. Black Dispossession and Affirmation
    3. The Second Coming of American Capital
    4. Impact on the Social Structure

| 7 | POLITICAL INDEPENDENCE AND NEO-COLONIALISM: 1962–1974 | 73 |

    1. Capitalist Development and JLP Repression
    2. Resistance to JLP Repression
    3. The Social Economy
    4. The State and Class Interests
    5. Political Parties and Class Interests

| 8 | DEMOCRATIC SOCIALISM, STRUGGLE AND CHANGE: 1974–1979 | 87 |

    1. Economic Crisis and the Response
    2. Resistance and Petit-Bourgeois Capitulation
    3. The Politics of Change, 1977-79
    4. Black Affirmation and Struggle
    5. The Class Basis of Zig-Zag Politics

CHAPTER		Page
9	THE STRUGGLE AHEAD: THE 1980 s	102

   1. Some Economic Facts on the Future of the Economy
   2. The Conjuncture at the Start of the 1980's
   3. Polarization of Class Forces

10	WHAT IS TO BE DONE: A SCENARIO FOR TRANSITION TO SOCIALISM	110

   1. The Political Economy of Transformation
   2. The Economic Horizon Just Ahead
   3. A Scenario to 2000 A.D.

EPILOGUE		125
APPENDIX	HISTORICAL DOCUMENTS	149

   1. The IMF, Democratic Socialism and Zig-Zag Politics: Jamaica, 1976-77 (Beckford, Nov. 1980)

   2. The Zigs and Zags of the Great Democratic Socialist Evolution (Witter, Sept. 1977)

BIBLIOGRAPHY	Suggested Further Readings	163

LIST OF DIAGRAMS

Diagram		Page
3.1	Model of a Colonial System	36
3.2	The Phases of Colonialism/Capitalism	37, 38
4.1	Post-Emancipation Social Structure of Jamaica	48
5.1	Schematic Representation of the Development of Class Struggle in Post-Emancipation Jamaica	60
6.1	Present Pattern of Social Stratification	71
8.1	Political Formations in Jamaica, 1979: Progress vs Reaction	97
8.2	Character of Multi-Class Party: PNP — Class and Organizational Structure	100
10.1	Proposed Administrative and Productive Organization for Socialist Transformation	120

LIST OF ABBREVIATIONS

ADC	Agricultural Development Corporation
ALCAN	Aluminum Company of Canada
BITU	Bustamante Industrial Trade Union
BOLAM	Bank of London and Montreal
CAST	College of Arts Science and Technology
CEO	Community Enterprise Organization
CFNI	Caribbean Food and Nutrition Institute (UWI)
CIA	Central Intelligence Agency (of the USA)
CMEA	Council for Mutual Economic Assistance
CPJ	Communist Party of Jamaica
DMWU	Dockers and Marine Workers Union
FAO	Food and Agriculture Organization (United Nations)
IBA	International Bauxite Association
IBRD	International Bank for Reconstruction and Development (World Bank)
IMF	International Monetary Fund
JAH	Jamaica Association of Higglers (JLP)
JALGO	Jamaica Association of Local Government Officers
JDB	Jamaica Development Bank
JIDC	Jamaica Industrial Development Corporation
JLP	Jamaica Labour Party
JMA	Jamaica Manufacturers Association
JPSCO	Jamaica Public Service Company
JSA	Jamaica School of Agriculture
KPH	Kingston Public Hospital
KSAC	Kingston and St. Andrew Corporation
MNC	Multinational Corporation
MNB	Multinational Bank
NIEO	New International Economic Order
NPM	National Patriotic Movement (JLP)
NWU	National Workers Union
OPEC	Organization of Petroleum Exporting Countries
PLL	Project Land Lease
PSOJ	Private Sector Organization of Jamaica
SEDCO	Small Enterprise Development Company
SEP	Special Employment Programme
STC	State Trading Corporation
TUC	Trade Union Congress

UAWU	University and Allied Workers Union
UBEC	Union of Banana Exporting Countries
UHWI	University Hospital of the West Indies
UTASP	Union of Technical, Administrative and Supervisory Personnel
U.W.I.	University of the West Indies
WFM	Womens Freedom Movement (JLP)
WIHC	West Indies Home Contractors
WLL	Workers Liberation League
WPJ	Workers Party of Jamaica
WSLB	Workers Savings and Loan Bank
YFNL	Youth Forces for National Liberation

PREFACE

Our intention in this book is to provide the reader with a deep understanding of the political economy of underdevelopment in Jamaica. We have written it in a way that it might be understood by all who read it.

The complete work consists of three separate publications: the book itself; an Appendix which was intended to be provided with the text, but which a publishing house like ours could not afford to print; and a statistical compendium to appear soon in the same form as the Appendix. The latter is the work of Witter and a team of students.

The decision to put out the historical documents in a separate pamphlet was painful. But printing costs are so high that it would raise the price of the book substantially. And that would defeat our purpose.

The Title

We were driving back to Town one day in 1975. Three of us in the waggon: my friend and painter man, Jango, from the West; my friend and university colleague, Louis Lindsay; with me (Beckford) at the wheel.

Quite naturally we got to philosophize about Jamaica and life on "the Rock". I cannot quite recall the exact sequence of exchange. But it was along the following lines:

Lindsay: What a beautiful country. Bwoy, if we could only correct the social ugliness.

Jango: Man, what a way only few man can get to enjoy God land and sea and sky. Dem big capitalist man have every ting. And so much a we too poor to feed we pickney and send dem to school. So much poor man wok so hard pon him lickle piece of ground. So much man have fe hustle fe live. Ah mi brethren "small garden but bitter weed".

Beckford: Sey dat again Jango. Me never hear dat one before.

Jango: Small garden but bitter weed.

Since that day this Jamaican folk statement remained locked in my head to be the title for whatever comprehensive analysis of our condition I would carry out in the future. This book is the first major effort since then. And its production arises from a sustained collaborative revolutionary intellectual campaign with Mikey Witter over the past 3½ years. It is truly a joint product.

The title captures the essence of the work. For the theme throughout the book is that since the European people invaded the New World and killed off the native Amerindian tribes throughout the Caribbean, white European capitalists have raped us Black people upside down, sideways, backways and every way.

They tore us from our roots in Africa, brought us forcibly and worked us too hard for us to enjoy the natural beauty of the Caribbean. They whipped us to work as slaves to amass fortunes from our labour. Then after we won our struggles against slavery, they continue to exploit our labour, take out the minerals from our land, destroy the natural fertility of the land growing sugar cane year in and year out for close to 400 years. They brain-washed our minds to think that everything African is inferior to anything European. Through education "Dan is the man" (Sparrow), "Crazy Ballheads" (Marley). Through advertising and the media. And through the entertainment we get.

Still the majority of our people (nearly all of us of African descent) are "too poor to enjoy what Jah (Nature) provides for Man".

Ah bwoy, donkey sey world no level. We inhabit a small garden, collectively and individually. But the bitter weed of King Sugar sprouts back in many forms of the same bitter weed of capitalism!

The Book

This book is intended to provide the kind of political educational ammunition to launch a final assault to eradicate the bitter weed of capitalism/imperialism, once and for all.

Our musical poets state our intention better than we ever could. Listen to the Wailers:

> "400 years, 400 years and
> it's the same philosophy
> I said it's 400 years, 400 years
> look how long
> And the people they still can't see ...
> Why do they fight against the poor youth of today

> Come on let's make the move ... make the move
> I say the time has come
> And if the fools don't see
> The youth is going to be strong
> So won't you come with me
> I will take you to a land of liberty
> Where we can live a good, good life
> And be free ..."

That is our purpose. To heighten further the level of consciousness of our people. To sharpen our intellectual machette to weed out the capitalist/imperialist bitter weed infesting our small garden — from the days of King Sugar to the present Multinational Corporations/Multinational Banks imperialist nexus with the 'fifth column' of national client capitalists.

Towards the end of the book, in the last chapter, we provide a scenario for building a socialist society rooted in the cultural tradition of our people. Then, and only then, we shall be in a position where our small garden will provide sweet fruit for all of us to partake.

We dedicate the book to the struggling youth of our Caribbean nation, of which Jamaica is but one parish. They are the majority of our people and they are the ones who will seize the time — when the right time come!

Brother Walter Rodney paid the ultimate price in preparing the ground for that time of liberation. And we dedicate the book to his loving memory.

Although our names appear as authors, the ideas expressed are the collective wisdom of a body of Caribbean (and other) scholars. They must share both the credit and the blame. Our position on this was stated by Rodney in his preface to *How Europe Under-developed Africa:*

> "I will not add that 'all mistakes and shortcomings are entirely my responsibility'. That is sheer bourgeois subjectivism. Responsibility in matters of these sorts is always collective, especially with regard to remedying the shortcomings." (pp. 7-8).

Several colleagues and friends gave us valuable comments and criticisms of the draft we circulated for a discussion session at which individual chapters were subjected to the scrutiny of selected persons. Kari Levitt gave us a detailed critical appraisal of the whole work. And Dalton McWheeny, a Jamaica School of Agriculture student, provided a critical layman's overview. Omar Davies reviewed Chapter 1. Richard Bernal, in addition to reviewing Chapters 2 and 3, made several other suggestions about improving the work. Don Robotham dealt incisively with Chapters 4 and 5. David Wong made some comments on Chapters 6 and 7. And Norman Girvan offered suggestions for improving Chapters 8, 9 and 10. In the general discussion, James Walsh, Wilberne Persaud and others gave helpful comments.

Last but not least, we record our appreciation of the typing skills of Audrey Wood and Joan Lofters, and for the type-setting of this book by Kathleen Miles.

G.B.
Mona, Jamaica
July, 1980

PREFACE TO REVISED EDITION

This revised edition is an improvement on the first "electoral and student" edition of October 1980. There are three substantive changes. First, Chapter 10 has been revised to provide an elaboration of the transition themes sketched in the first edition. Secondly, we have written an "Epilogue" which analyses the electoral defeat of Manley's PNP and the character and policies of the new JLP regime. Thirdly, we include one of the two historical documents as an Appendix. Production costs prohibit inclusion of the other document to which we refer in the introductory note.

September 16, 1981   GB

CHAPTER 1

PEOPLE, SOCIETIES AND CHANGE – THE STUDY OF POLITICAL ECONOMY

A basic premise of our study is that society, together with the natural environment, constitutes the objective, or material, reality which exists outside of us. As such, society, or social reality, is a proper object for scientific enquiry. The scientific method is the mode of human thought that has been used very successfully in discovering the inner truths of material reality or Nature. The scientific method applied to the study of society is known as *historical materialism*. This is the method we will use to investigate the interconnections and interplay between the struggles of our peoples and the development of our society. As the natural scientist seeks to discover nature's physical laws in order to utilize natural forces on man's behalf, so the social scientist seeks the inner laws of the development of society in order to use the social forces to change society.

In adopting a scientific approach we do not assert either that we can explain all aspects of reality – nor especially that other perspectives do not shed light on how our society came to be what it is, and how it is to be transformed. For social reality has many sides, each with its own peculiarities. The perspective we offer is but a framework for social analysis which can serve as a point of departure for more specialized and detailed analysis. More than that, we offer it as a positive contribution to the national dialogue among the progressive and patriotic masses of Jamaicans.

Through the lens of historical materialism, society is seen to be a dynamic whole, a unity of inter-connected parts, in a constant process of change. Every society has an irreversible history, a historically determined present, and a future. The future, like the present and the past before it, is determined by the outcome of individual and collective human action within the historically given social reality; and of course the independent evolution of the natural environment itself. Most of the time these changes, social and natural, occur gradually, even imperceptibly. Often times, social changes are abrupt and violent; this is revolutionary change as opposed to evolutionary change. Revolution, in this sense, is a heightening of the tempo of social change (which is always going on) at a particular point in history.

The process of social change is never random or haphazard, though it may appear so. Instead social change proceeds by way of principles or (scientific) laws, just as an egg hatches into a chick according to its own internal laws; or just as a boy becomes a man according to the laws of human biology. To say that social change is a law-governed process appears to imply that human action is predetermined and ordained as if by fate. But as we will show below, these laws derive out of human action/interaction in society, as well as human action on Nature. The task of the philosopher and social scientist is to discover and understand these laws. The task of the revolutionary is to use these laws to change society. The demise of the adventurist and of reformists dreaming of utopias and ideal societies is that they ignore the historically given laws which govern social change.

The source of change is always the action of human beings, but action conditioned by their natural and social environment. "Men make history, but they do not do so as they wish" [Marx]. In societies which are divided into classes, such as capitalist society, people's actions are primarily determined by their class background and class outlook. Some classes, such as masters and slaves and capitalists and workers, stand in antagonistic contradiction to each other, meaning that one class maintains and reproduces itself at the expense of the other. The working out (or resolution) of antagonistic contradictions constitutes the principal source of change.

1. The Anatomy of Society

No society can exist unless its members are able to procure their means of survival — food, clothing, shelter, etc. In fact, society begins when human beings enter into definite relations among themselves, consciously and willingly or otherwise, in order to carry out the social production of their means of survival. In some simple societies, in antiquity as well as in isolated places in the modern world, land is the principal means of producing society's needs and is collectively owned. Enshrined in the customs of these societies are well determined rules governing the relationships among members during the planting, reaping and distribution of the products of the land and the people's labour. Likewise in slave societies, some are enslaved by others, the masters, in order that the slaves produce goods and services for the master. In capitalist society, there are propertyless workers with nothing to sell but their ability and capacity to work; on the other hand, there are capitalists who own the means of production — land, raw materials, machines, tools, buildings and so forth — and can afford to hire workers to produce goods for them.

Notice that in all cases the people are bound together in order to carry out production. The villagers must co-operate if they are to cultivate sufficient land, and harvest it to provide for the needs of everybody. There can be no masters if there are no slaves, and conversely. Nor can some be capitalists unless there are workers who by virtue of being propertyless (i.e. they own no means of production) have to work for them. Of foremost importance in the study of society are the *relations of production* — the social relations between people in the process of production that dominate and characterize the society.

There are two principal kinds of relations of production. On the one hand, there are *technical relations* which arise from the technical division of labour in production. Thus, there is a technical relation between two workers on an assembly line in so far as their functions and tasks depend on each other. Similarly, there is a technical relation between the truck driver and the crane operator in the loading of, say, bauxite ore for transportation to the docks. That is, their functions depend on each other or complement each other in the process of production. On the other hand, there are *property relations* which arise on the basis of individual ownership of things. Thus the landlord establishes a relation between himself and his cultivator tenant when he rents him land. Similarly, there is a relationship established between the capitalist owner of the factory and the worker operating the capitalist's machine.

In the final analysis, production is really a struggle between man and the rest of Nature to wrest the fruits of Nature for man's subsistence. Man is constantly transforming Nature, often by using some of Nature's forces against others.

For example, the force of gravity and the strength of the sledge hammer increases the power of the man to overcome the stone's resistance and crush it. Likewise, the fisherman might use wind to sail his boat on the oceans. In the process of transforming Nature, however, man is himself transformed. For example, the ditch digger gets stronger muscles; the industrial worker acquires the knowledge of tools, the materials and the production process in which he works; the farmer learns the seasons and the properties of the soil; the fisherman learns the signs for changes in the weather, and so on.

By *means of production* we mean the tools, machines, materials, buildings, land, etc., which increase man's capacity to act on and transform Nature. It is on the basis of ownership of the means of production that property relations are established among people. Private property has not always existed nor will it always exist. Like everything else it came into being at some time, developed and will pass away. In some societies, land and other means of production are collectively owned. In others, such as slave, and capitalist societies, ownership is concentrated in the hands of a few. Thus, we observe that groups of people who have a common, but definite, relation to the means of production constitute a *class*.

For example, landlords are the class of people who own land and live off the rental income of their property. Peasants are farmers who either own land or rent small portions of land. In either case, the farmer relies primarily on the labour of himself and his family, supplemented with a few hired labourers, particularly at planting and harvesting times. Capitalists own wealth, which may take the form of money, or means of production and which is used to hire workers as wage labourers. Workers, or wage labourers, own no means of production, and in this sense they are propertyless. Being propertyless, they have nothing else to sell but their labour power — their capacity to work — to those who will and can buy it, usually the capitalists or the state.

Apart from bearing a common relation to the means of production, and by extension sharing a common place in the production process, members of a social class generally share other class characteristics: housing location and conditions, culture and sometimes race, ideology and politics. Furthermore, some classes stand in antagonistic contradiction to each other; that is, one class on the basis of its ownership of the means of production, is able to exploit the labour of the propertyless. We can therefore express property relations among people more precisely as relations between classes arising out of the basis of ownership of the means of production. It is the dominant property relations in any society which "cast a shadow or hue" on all other social relations and which ultimately account for the character of society and its mode of development.

The relations of production, including the property relations, are themselves determined by the level of development of the *forces of production*. What do we mean by the forces of production? We mean society's capacity to act on and transform Nature in the process of production. Consider the task of digging irrigation canals. It can be done with sharp sticks, metal hoes and shovels, or modern bulldozers. Each technique represents a different level of man's capacity to dig canals, starting from the most backward to the most modern. The means of production by themselves are useless. But together with the skills and experience of an organized labour force raw materials can be produced and processed to satisfy human wants and needs. In other words, the means of production and the collective skill, technology and labour-power constitute society's *forces of production*.

The collection of the means of production never remains the same. Some are worn out in the production process. Others are produced to replace and displace existing means of production. As new and better means of production are produced and as workers get more skills and experiences and their numbers increase, society can produce more and more in any given period of time. Thus the level of development of the forces of production grows or increases.

Earlier, it was suggested that there are different types of social relations of production characterizing different societies. In slave society, production was carried out by the master-slave relation; in capitalist society, production is carried out by the capitalist-worker relation, and so on. Given any set of productive forces with a given level of development, some types of social relations will be appropriate and others will not. For example, modern production of high precision tools requiring skill, ingenuity and creative initiative could not be carried on by slaves kept in ignorance and trained only in simple tasks. The production of computers would not make sense using slave labour. Large scale cultivation is not possible where land is widely owned and fragmented into many small plots.

Similarly, in a situation where land was relatively abundant as in Jamaica in the seventeenth century, English planters would have had to offer extremely high wages to attract labour from the obvious alternative of independent small farming. Hence, in order to produce sugar cane on plantations with a highly labour intensive technique, Africans imported into Jamaica were enslaved so as to deny them the opportunity for alternative and independent employment. After slavery was abolished, indentureship was a form of contract used to bind East Indians and Chinese who were brought here to replace Africans on the estates. So that even though the planters came from capitalist Europe, they made slaves, not wage-earners (workers or proletariat) out of Africans.

We refer to the combination of productive forces and the characteristic social relations of production appropriate to these forces as the *mode of production*. It is, in a sense, the material basis of society. The mode of production determines what is produced, how it is produced and distributed and for whose benefit. Jamaican society was based on a slave mode of production, although of a peculiar kind, until Emancipation. Thereafter, there emerged a capitalist mode of production and an independent peasant mode of production, with the latter ultimately being subordinated by the former. The contradictions between these two modes lies at the basis of the struggles of the Jamaican people since 1838.

Society, however, is much more than a mode of production. There is usually a legal system, a state, culture, religion, the people's ideas as well as other types of social relations such as kinship and family relations, relations between professionals and clients, ordinary friendships and so on. That is, there is an immense array of different types of social relations among people, other than relations of production, which are obvious to everyone and which are commonly understood to constitute the fabric of society. This complex of social relations, outside of the mode of production, is called the *superstructure* of society as opposed to the base, the mode of production — in particular, the characteristic property relations within the mode — on which the superstructure rests. A society, or a *social formation,* therefore consists of two principal parts: a mode of production and a superstructure.

Not any superstructure will be appropriate to a given mode of production. Obviously a slave mode of production cannot have in its superstructure a legal system which forbids slavery. Similarly, the dominant ethics, values and laws of a capitalist society must sanction and protect the right of individuals (meaning capitalists) to own and dispose of their property as they wish. Where the superstructure does not complement, but is in contradiction to, the mode of production, the society. is inherently unstable. Such may be the case in periods of transition from one type of social formation to another.

2. The Dynamics of Social Change

Above, we asserted that society was a dynamic, ever changing reality, which develops according to its own internal laws as a result of the working out of contradictions, principally class contradictions, within society itself. We can go further in our explanation of social change at a general level. The struggle between man and the rest of Nature, which is called production, generates a tendency to raise the level of development of society's productive forces. In other words, as human beings accumulate more and more knowledge about their natural environment from their experiences in production, they learn to solve more problems and increase their capacity to transform Nature to suit human needs. Better tools are designed using hardier materials (metals), more efficient techniques are developed, more powerful sources of energy are trapped and so on. Notice we said that there was a tendency for the struggle between man and Nature to raise the level of development of the social productive forces. However, there may be countervailing tendencies from outside the particular society — from some other society — to stagnate and retard the growth of the productive forces. This is properly a part of our enquiry. Alternatively, violent natural changes may destroy some of society's productive forces and thus weaken society's capacity to transform Nature. For example, an earthquake may destroy an irrigation canal and dam system, thereby undermining agricultural productivity. Similarly, a hurricane may destroy buildings, power facilities and so on.

Notice also that elements within the superstructure, such as people's collective knowledge, improved language and communication, etc., strengthen man in his struggle with Nature. Conversely, poor work attitudes inherited from the old society, laws preventing the redistribution of land, prejudices against new techniques of management and production, etc., tend to weaken man's productive capacity and undermine development of the forces of production. In this, as well as other ways the superstructure impinges upon the mode of production and facilitates or retards the development of the productive forces.

As the level of development of the productive forces increases, the old relations of production become less and less appropriate; thereby becoming more and more a "fetter" on further growth. For example, modern capitalist industry requires the availability of a pool of labour from which it can draw its labour power, as well as access to large amounts of capital. A society where the dominant property relations are such that each man had his own tools, workshop, access to raw materials and so forth, could not undertake large scale manufacturing. What is historically required is that independent producers be separated from their means of production to force them to sell their labour power in order to secure the means of survival for their families. Simultaneously, their many small individual capitals have to be concentrated in the hands of a few individual capitalists who can undertake the quantum of investment required by modern large scale manufacturing. Thus, the relations of production while formerly facilitating the growth of the productive forces becomes an obstacle to further development and must therefore be changed.

Historically, all such changes are revolutionary and result in much social dislocation. For changes in social relations mean changes in the relative positions of the classes within the society; some classes may even be abolished, such as when landlords are expropriated. Those classes with a vested interest in the old order of society will always defend the *status quo* — the way things are — and fight against classes which are oppressed under the old order and which stand to benefit from a new order of society. But soon, the new relations of production that are established begin to facilitate and encourage the growth of the productive forces and society moves to a qualitatively higher level of development.

So far we have identified two sets of contradictions. The first between man and the rest of Nature, the resolution (through struggle) of which engenders the second: the contradiction between the forces of production and the relations of production. The second in turn, in the process of its resolution, engenders yet a third contradiction: namely, the contradiction between the base and the superstructure. For with the mode of production changing, partly under the influence of the superstructure, the latter in turn must also adjust to the new mode of production. The superstructural changes — new governments, new laws, new institutions, etc. — are phenomenal political manifestations of deeper changes within the society. And if we are to get the fullest understanding, we must get to the bottom of things and analyse the nature and causes of the underlying changes in society's base.

The analysis above can be put in the form of a simple scheme which shows society at various levels of development. Each stage would be characterized by a qualitatively distinct social formation based on its characteristic mode of production and superstructure. At each stage of development, the society includes elements of earlier social formations which have passed away, as well as the seeds for new formations coming into being.

Above we have outlined briefly the approach of historical materialism to the society. It is historical in so far as it seeks to understand the present in terms of the development of its history. It is materialist in so far as it seeks the explanation of social phenomenon in underlying material causes. It is dialectical in so far as it considers everything to be in a process of dialectical change; that is, change resulting from the working out of opposing forces in contradiction to each other within society itself. That is why in this view, "class struggle is the motive force of history", for it is in the contention among classes for wealth and power that the contradictions, just identified, express themselves.

We have outlined the method of study in its most general form. We will need to be more specific in analysing the particular development of Jamaican society within the general development of the world as a whole. In doing so we will have to recognize these additional factors. First, relations among societies influence the development of those societies. This seems to say that external causes account for changes in society, in apparent contradiction of what was stated earlier. But what is really meant is that external forces when they impinge on society, interact with the internal dynamic of the particular society. That is in the internal struggle between the classes, external forces alternatively strengthen one or the other of the classes; and, thereby, work through its particular laws of motion. At times therefore, when we view world society as a whole, all social forces will be internal, the only external forces being Natural forces. At other times when we consider Jamaican society, we cannot do so as if it were isolated but must take account of external, natural, as well as social forces.

Second, we must take account of racial oppression and its ideology, racism. Here, we shall argue that race relations reflect underlying class contradictions within society; and we shall demonstrate the role of institutionalized racial oppression in the development of Jamaican society. This will be a principal example of how certain elements within the superstructure of society namely racism and unequal race relations, impinge upon and affect the mode of production, both positively and negatively. That it may have a positive influence on the development of the mode of production is another way of saying that it has negative dehumanizing consequences for the oppressed as well as their oppressors. Conversely, when it begins to undermine the mode of production, as in Jamaica in the 18th and 19th centuries, and in Zimbabwe and Southern Africa in the 1970's, "then comes the era of social revolution" and the way is cleared for "turning the table on the slavemaster".

Third, when we treat of individuals we will be concerned not only with how they affect history, but also in what ways they too are a product of their history. In this context we will have occasion to touch upon the socio-psychological aspects of oppression and struggle in Jamaica — both past and present. An important theme is that alienation — psychological as well as cultural — is essentially a response to oppression. Ultimately, this reflects the philosophical outlook which sees man's social consciousness as determined by his social being. Put another way, material existence is the source of thought; matter is the source of spirit.

CHAPTER 2

FROM EUROPEAN CONQUEST TO EMANCIPATION

Toward the end of the fifteenth century, powerful social and economic forces were developing in Europe — especially England — which completed the disintegration of feudal society and initiated a process of European expansionism. This expansionism eventually took the form of colonization whereby vast areas of the world and its peoples were subjugated. In the vanguard of this expansion were merchant adventurers searching for precious metals and luxury goods. They were backed by the power of princes and monarchs eager to fill their treasuries with gold and silver, and to extend the prestige of their realms.

Merchant profit is the difference between buying low (or otherwise acquiring goods cheaply) and selling high. The further the market from the source of supply, and the higher the luxury status attached to the commodity, the greater the profit on the merchant's capital outlay. Thus the merchants took to the high seas; or they financed pirates and brigands, like Columbus and Drake, to find new routes to the silks and spices of the Far East. The ancient land routes had long been monopolized by Italian and Arab merchants. If in the search for a sea route, gold and silver could be found along the way, so much the better.

1. Conquest of the Americas

Among the first to be conquered and colonized in this period were the societies of the Americas, or what to the Europeans was the New World. At this time in history, when contact was first made with the Europeans, some societies of the Americas were backward and tribal whereas others, such as those of Highland America — from Mexico to Peru — were highly advanced and sophisticated civilizations. The invading European societies, though still in the infancy of capitalism, were more advanced than even the empires of the Incas, Mayas and Aztecs in the technology of military and naval warfare. In other spheres — for example, aspects of culture and social organization — the Europeans were still relatively backward compared to the Incas and Aztecs.

In the Caribbean — as well as other lowland parts of the Americas — Amerindian[1] society was quite backward. It was based on a communal mode of production in which resources were communally utilized on behalf of the whole society. Private property — in the means of production — was unknown. Primarily, the people engaged in hunting, fishing and shifting (slash and burn) agriculture. The *fruits* of production were distributed according to well defined rules laid down in tradition. Production was never much more than subsistence level, with a small surplus to support the elite class of non-producers — priests, elders, and those who specialized in warfare and the knowledge of science. For the Europeans, these simple societies were no match. Nor were the Amerindian civilizations of the Aztec, Maya or Inca empires able to withstand the onslaught of the Europeans — although in many respects they had achieved higher levels of technology than the conquering Europeans.

European conquest meant, in the first place, the plunder and looting of the gold and precious metals. This was especially so under Spanish colonialism which lasted in Jamaica until the middle of the 17th century. This was one phase of the initial ("primitive") accumulation of wealth which Marx described vividly: "The discovery of gold and silver in America, the extirpation, enslavement and entombment in mines of the aboriginal population, the beginning of the conquest and looting of the East Indies, the turning of Africa into a warren for the commercial hunting of black-skins, signalized the rosy dawn of the era of capitalist production".

The quotation refers to the fact that the colonization of America was part of a world-wide process. Africa and Asia eventually also fell under the heel of the European exploiters. It was a process which led to massive depopulation of large parts of the Americas, including Jamaica; and the subsequent repopulation with colonized peoples from Africa and Asia, and migrant European settlers.

Colonization destroyed the indigenous society, primarily by killing off the population and hence the labour force.

---

[1] It has been brought to our attention that the classification of indigenous Americans as "Indians" reflected the European's belief that they had arrived in India. Thus, the terms *West Indians* and *Amerindian*.

Through forced labour, the transmission of foreign diseases, wanton murder, and suicide induced by the fear of impending destruction, the Arawak population was rapidly eliminated. So complete was this destruction that the subsequent history and culture of the Jamaican people revealed not even the slightest trace of Arawak influence. In varying degrees the Indian societies of the Americas shared a similar fate to the Arawaks. Thus, today in South and Central America, the impoverished remnants of the once brilliant Amerindian civilizations live in destitution and poverty.

2. English Colonization

In 1655, England captured Jamaica from Spain and a new era in colonization was opened. After one and a half centuries of Spanish rule, the population was only a few thousand, the majority of whom were African, or a mixture of Spanish, African and in some cases Arawak Indian. The Arawak population, estimated to have been once as high as 60,000 had all but disappeared. From as early as 1517, Africans had been brought as household slaves to tend to the personal needs of their Spanish masters. However, there were never many of them as the back-breaking labour on the Spanish farms and in the mines was done by the Arawaks, at the ultimate cost of their lives.

The Spanish colonialists had already appropriated much of the land and natural resources which the Arawaks had traditionally used in communal production. With the destruction of the population, only the land passed into the control of the English.

The remnants of the population which had survived — retreated to the interior of the island to pursue a life of hunting and small farming. Thus, the basis was laid for the development of two types of society: on the one hand there was the subsistence economy of the Maroons — mainly Africans — who took to the hills; on the other, the English settlers established what later became *slave plantation society*.

Until 1739 when the Treaty recognizing a limited and superficial independence for the Maroons was signed, there was constant guerilla warfare between the English and the Maroons. On the one hand, this led to a precarious survival for the Maroons' subsistence economy with so much time and manpower spent in fighting and eluding the colonialists. On the other hand, the Maroon raids inflicted severe damages to English farms and plantations and, of course, loss of life. The main issues of Maroon struggles were the defence of their freedom, and the right to their lands to ensure their economic survival. Thus the Arawak resistance to colonialism was continued by the Maroons, who became early masters of guerilla warfare. The Maroon resistance, and the quasi-independence it won them, have symbolized the struggle for freedom and independence throughout subsequent Jamaican history. Nevertheless, there was another aspect of the Maroons which led them to collaborate with the English to maintain their African brothers in captivity.

English colonial production began with settlers on small family farms. These settlers arrived not only from England but also from other English colonies such as Barbados. Like most colonial settlers they were uprooted persons, outcasts and misfits and in general those who could not make a satisfactory living in England. In several respects, they were victims of the process of transition to capitalism, which wrenched them from their customary roles in feudal society and threw them in the cities as cheap labour for the factories of the emergent capitalism. There were also of course, colonial administrators and wealthy merchants who commuted between the mother country and the colony.

At first, the settlers grew a variety of food crops. Soon however, high quality cane introduced from Barbados made sugar cane production extremely profitable. One by one, the small farms were gobbled up and concentrated in large sugar cane plantations. Large-scale sugar cane production required a large, cheap, labour force. With the Arawaks wiped out, the few Maroons determined to be free, the only other domestic source of labour was the dispossessed Europeans. Apparently it would have been too expensive to induce Europeans to labour on plantations by paying wages which was the characteristic way of obtaining labour under (European) capitalism. This was especially so since the Europeans had the options of striking out anew on virgin Crown land or going back home.

3. Slave Plantation Society

The solution to the labour problem was found in African slaves. The Portuguese had already established a trade in

African slaves which was quite profitable. Envious of these profits, as capitalists always are, and in need of labour for its sugar-cane colonies, English merchants actively entered the slave trade in the mid-16th century with the establishment of the Royal Africa Company. And in the end, established England as the major slave trading nation. The immense importance of the profits from the slave trade in fuelling the Industrial Revolution and in the development of merchant capitalism has been studied thoroughly — notably by Walter Rodney and Eric Williams. In a later chapter, we return to this.

By the late 17th century, the English began importing a large number of slaves for sale to the planters. For the next 150 years Jamaica was a slave plantation society, specialising in the production of sugar cane for export to England. Capital in the form of finance to purchase slaves and other inputs were supplied by English merchants, while all goods imported into the colony arrived exclusively in English ships. The fundamental relation between the English merchant and the planter was a client-debtor relation. Ultimately it was the indebtedness of the planters to the merchants which ensured the fall of the planter class.

Plantation society was based on a slave mode of production. This meant that production was organized by a class of property-owners who owned not only the land and other means of production but slaves as well.

These slaves were then put to work under the strict supervision of drivers armed with whips, and the fruits of their labours belonged entirely to the slave-masters. In return, the slaves were fed cheap rations to replenish their energies, just as if they were draught animals. Thus the fundamental social relations through which production was carried out was inherently contradictory: on the one hand there were white European slave masters; on the other hand, there were the black African slaves whom they exploited mercilessly.

But it was a slave mode spawned and dominated by English capitalism. The purpose of production was private profit, and for the capitalists there was no limit to the amount of profit they wanted. Thus where higher production levels meant higher profits, it also meant an intensification of the exploitation of the slaves — longer hours, many lashes to speed up the pace of work, and more lashes for any reason the drivers could find. The slave mode was totally dependent on the English market: it was supplied with inputs from English factories and in turn sold its output to English consumers. The planters were forever indebted to big English merchant houses and in reality functioned as mere agents for them. Thus the reproduction of slave society from year to year depended on its relations with English capitalism and the latter expanded on the surpluses thus extracted from slave production.

This basic antagonistic and contradictory social relation between European capitalist slave-master and African slave was reflected in all other spheres of society and left a lasting impression on subsequent Jamaican history.

The social stratification within the society reflected the stratification within the plantation. That is, white European capitalist plantation owners and managers stood at the pinnacle of society with Black African slaves at the lowest level of the social order. Over time — as a result of the physical rape of the African slave women — there developed in between these two classes the Brown mulatto class of "Free Coloureds" who served from their inception as a buffer (or broker) between the two principal classes. This rigid pattern of social stratification did not permit any social mobility within the society for the enslaved African. Only by escape could he survive as a Maroon.

Slave plantation economy was segmented in that there was very little economic exchange between the plantations, since they were all producing the same thing. Generally, the plantations depended on a small group of local merchants and shippers for their import and export needs. (These local merchants were in reality hardly more than agents for English-based merchant houses). Further, each plantation strove to be self-sufficient, producing as far as possible the inputs (tools, farm equipment, etc.) and services (blacksmith, carpenter, etc.) it required. Thus while there was little or no exchange among plantations, there was an extensive division of labour within the plantation which necessitated an exchange of functions, tasks and products, though not market exchange.

The plantation was a total institution in so far as it provided for all permissible needs for the slaves and dominated their existence totally, from birth to death. The plantation — like the prison or the asylum — transformed all who entered its gates. Thus African peasants were put through a process of seasoning whereby they would be transformed into hardy and obedient slaves. The process of reculturization was promoted by the deliberate mixing of slaves from different tribes while suppressing all cultural symbols and relations, even language. One result was the development of a pidginised version of the master's English language, which permitted communication among slaves and between the slave and planter classes. Another result was the use of song as a medium for articulating resistance to the oppression and as an outlet for the physical and psychological pain of the slave master's whip. For the roots of mento, calypso, and reggae reach back into slavery where social criticism and satire could only be expressed in song. Slave masters then (as their successor capitalist classes now) were incapable of feeling the message of song, and often never tried to understand.

4. Emancipation: Class Struggles in Jamaica and England

Oppression of any form and anywhere breeds the appropriate resistance. Slave resistance took many forms: sabotage, withdrawal of labour ("laziness"), protest in words and in song, escape and outright rebellion. In this situation the class contradictions forced the white planter class to develop instruments of military coercion in order to minimize rebellions and to prevent revolutions. The principal responsibility for maintaining slave society and containing the inherent contradictions belonged to the colonial state headed by the Governor. At various times, differences developed between the planters and the colonial government; but toward the fundamental task of keeping the Africans enslaved there was a total unity of interests.

All the historical evidence shows that the slaves resisted militantly and otherwise sought to subvert and undermine slave society. Everywhere in the colonial world there were revolts and rebellions. Notable among these struggles were the Berbice revolution of 1763 in Guyana and the San Domingo revolution towards the end of the 18th century. In

Jamaica, in particular we should recall the Christmas Rebellion of 1831 led by Sam Sharpe. The success of the Haitian revolution gave extra impetus to slave rebellions elsewhere in the region; and planter government's military control of the situation became increasingly expensive and tenuous.

In 1804 the heroic struggles of the slaves in Haiti against French colonialism was consummated with the establishment of the first independent black nation in the Americas. The revolution had drawn some of its inspiration from the struggles of the working people in the French revolution of 1789. They rallied behind the slogan of "liberty, equality and fraternity" for all. As it turned out, the bourgeoisie, in classical fashion, usurped political power from the old feudal ruling class weakened by the upheavals of the peasants and artisans. In the bourgeois conception of liberty, equality and fraternity applied to men of property — namely themselves. This is why the French revolution marks the birth of capitalism in France. The slaves in Haiti, however, interpreted the slogan even more broadly than the French working classes. They interpreted it to mean freedom of the slaves as well.

The revolution also drew inspiration from the struggles of the Maroons in Jamaica as well. In Toussaint's army were Maroons who had fled Jamaica by canoe to Haiti. With the triumph of the revolution, the English slavemasters in Jamaica began to fear that their slaves too would follow the example of their Haitian brothers and rise up in bloody revolution. (Thus, there is historical precedence for the fear of the Jamaican ruling class about the lessons of the "Cuban model").

This fear was to prove justified as the Jamaican slave rebellion and revolt intensified, culminating in the Sam Sharpe led Christmas rebellion of 1831. Gripped by the fear of impending disaster and undermined by the loss of political power to the industrial bourgeoisie, the English merchant-planters could no longer contain the struggles of the slaves. In this way, the English, French and Haitian class struggles fed into the Jamaican class struggle and dictated the Emancipation of the slaves.

One of the principal means of social control which complemented the military establishment of the colonial state was the principle of divide and rule. It was systematically applied to the slave population so as to keep them dis-united and reduce the possibility of successful rebellion. Not only were slaves on different estates segregated from each other, but on each estate potential leaders were isolated out and sometimes traded. In addition, the system of hierarchy created social divisions among the slaves. Thus, more often than not, drivers were African slaves of a different tribe from those they "drove". In addition, there were special house slaves[2] chosen primarily on the basis of their loyalty to the master to tend to the personal needs of himself and his family. Often these were mulatto offspring of the planter and his administrators. Many a revolt was nipped in the bud by planters acting on tips from slaves treacherous to their own class and loyal to the master. Again, Sam Sharpe's rebellion exemplified this.

Yet another example of the tactics of divide and rule was the transformation of the Maroons from freedom fighters into a force for catching runaway slaves. On the one hand the very existence of Africans in *maronnage*, fighting to maintain their limited freedom and independence was a constant source of inspiration and symbol of the negation of slavery. Thus slaves were forever escaping to join the simple hunting and farming society. In many cases, however, they were returned to their masters by the Maroons. This had been part of the conditions of peace in the treaty between the English and the Maroons in 1739. Years of guerilla warfare and struggle with the superior English military force had incessantly disrupted Maroon society, with the result that production in some places was never more than subsistence level and often much less than that. In their eagerness to maintain freedom and independence in peace for themselves they served the counter-revolutionary role of assisting the planters in maintaining their African brothers in slavery.

Finally, from the beginning of the slave plantation in mid-17th century a division among Africans between slaves and free blacks began to develop. Some of these were freed slaves. The majority were the mulatto offspring of the planter class, many of whom had acquired small but substantial property in land, cattle and even slaves. Others became

---

[2] Malcolm X once defined the house-slave as the one who seeing his master's house on fire cries out "Master *our* house is on fire".

preachers, teachers, and businessmen. This class of free blacks played from its inception, a dual and contradictory role. At times, it sought to articulate the demands of the masses — in this period, the slaves — and to unite them in a struggle against the colonialists for their rights. But as soon as this unity started to develop, they would switch to tactics of confusion and of dividing the masses out of a deep fear that if the masses turn the oppressive society upside down, they the mulatto middle class might be swept away as well. We mention this phenomenon here in passing, but will return to it in a later chapter. There we will discuss its pervasiveness throughout subsequent Jamaican history under the rubric of "Middle Class Politics".

Slave society lasted until 1838, the year of formal but, we argue, substantially incomplete emancipation. Already in 1807, the slave trade itself had been abolished. The hey-day of sugar was during the 17th-18th centuries. True, there were many ups and downs as production costs rose and favourable market conditions weakened. From the end of the 17th century on, sugar production survived under the protection of tariffs levied on sugar produced outside the English colonial empire.

Slave society, however, could not weather for long the internal class struggles between the planters and slaves, nor the impact of profound qualitative changes in English capitalism. With respect to the latter, as capitalism developed there arose a class of industrial capitalists who usurped the dominant role which the merchants had enjoyed. Increasingly, merchant capital came to serve the needs of industrial capital by distributing its products; and in doing so became subordinated to it. Prior to that, it was merchant capital which had financed the initial industrial system — the so-called "putting-out" system, whereby craftsmen were supplied with materials by merchants to produce goods for them. But now, merchant capital was to be eclipsed by industrial capital.

In this struggle the ideologues and spokesmen for the rising industrial bourgeoisie championed the cause of emancipation of the slaves. Despite the moralistic character of their arguments, ultimately their case rested on the inefficiency of slave production compared with European small farmer production of beet sugar. For the industrial capitalists, cheaper sugar and grain meant cheaper wage goods and hence lower wage bills. Thus they inveighed heavily against slave production for its inefficiency meant lower profits for the industrial bourgeoisie. As the pressure from the mother country for the abolition of slavery developed and reinforced the internal class struggles within the colony, the system began to crumble. It was left for the colonialists to design a strategy for accommodating the inherent internal tensions and contradictions. The strategy was to formally emancipate the slaves but deny them real freedom by ensuring that the means of production, particularly land, remained in the hands of European capitalists. Burdened by debts and taxes and unable to acquire land of their own, the former slaves were forced by economic circumstances to sell their labour-power for wages, usually to the same planter who had previously exploited them as slaves. Change, without change — yet another recurrent theme throughout our history of struggles.

But before we go any further with the story of Jamaican economic and social development through the struggles of the people, we must pause to examine developments within Europe and particularly England. It is here that we locate the political and economic roots of colonization, subsequently the world capitalist economy. Plantation Jamaica was a product of the revolutionary social changes in Europe which had been gathering momentum for centuries.

CHAPTER 3

EUROPEAN CAPITALISM, COLONIALISM AND IMPERIALISM

Capitalism, as a qualitatively distinct social system, is relatively new in human history. The capitalist mode of production was first established in England in the 17th century principally in the form of agrarian capitalism. Tenant farmers and landowners increasingly employed wage labour (farm hands) to produce and market crops and livestock (sheep) for sale at a profit. The old feudal relationships prevalent during the Middle Ages were undermined. During and after the English Revolution of 1640-68, political power passed from feudal nobles and the monarchy to the new classes of capitalist landlords, large farmers and city merchants.

Capitalism passed through three main stages: mercantilism (1648-1760), industrial capitalism (1760-1870) and monopoly capitalism (1870-?). Modern colonialism has been the hand-maiden of capitalism, always adjusting to its changing needs. In doing so colonial development reflected the qualitative development of European capitalism.

1. Mercantile Capitalism

Throughout Europe, the growth of long distance trade facilitated and, in turn, was stimulated by the rise of the merchant class. In the early pre-industrial stage of capitalism, capital was accumulated principally from the profits of long distance and overseas trade. Successful merchants became Europe's principal bankers and money lenders. The landed nobility was frequently driven to bankruptcy by a combination of outrageous interest rates and their greed in desiring to purchase silks, spices and other luxuries brought from the far corners of the world by the merchants, while exploiting and neglecting their manorial estates.

In return for financing the metropolitan state and enabling it to build navies and armies, the merchants received privileges and monopolies whereby they could act as effective colonial authorities in the Far East, the coast of Africa and the sectors of the New World.

The merchants from the sea-faring nations of Holland, Spain and Portugal were relatively advanced in shipping and navigation and took the lead in finding new sea routes to the rich markets of the East. In the process, the Americas were colonized and the first stage of modern colonialism was opened. But though the merchants of these countries had accumulated vast amounts of wealth, particularly from the colonies, it was in England that mercantile capitalism first established itself.

The first stage of colonialism followed the Spanish/Portuguese voyages in search of sea routes to the East. The routes over land had long been monopolized by the trading cities of the Mediterranean — e.g. Venice, Genoa, etc. — and the Moslems of the Middle East. From the 13th century, Crusades, blessed and sanctioned by the Popes, had been mounted in a vain attempt to break the monopoly of Moslem traders. The religious justification for mobilizing armies of crusaders was to wrest the Holy Land from the infidels, as the Moslems were called by the Catholic Church. In 1492, Columbus sailed into the Caribbean and thought he had reached India; hence the misnomer, "West Indies". In 1497, Vasco da Gama, the Portuguese explorer, rounded the Cape of Good Hope at the tip of southern Africa and then headed north. In a real sense, this symbolized the birth of the world economy.

These voyages had been organized by companies of merchants, with the support of the Kings. The guiding purpose was to secure luxury goods cheaply from the East for resale at a profit to the European ruling classes. But here in the Americas they found gold and silver, which in the mercantilist outlook was the essence of wealth. Though they claimed the territories in the names of the Pope and the Kings, these colonies were more immediately the property of the merchant companies.

The first stage of colonialism took the form of direct company rule. The merchants plundered the colony and seized existing wealth, whether in natural form, produced by the indigenous people of the colony, or pirated from other traders on the high seas. Thus Mexico and Peru were drained of their gold and silver. Other colonies, like Jamaica, with little or no precious metals, served as strategic outposts for the refitting of the metropole's ships. In this stage of colonialism, there was no real attempt to reorganize production within the colony with the exception of the use of forced labour in the mines. This was a form of what Marx called *primitive accumulation* [of capital]. That is, it was a form of accumulating wealth from pre-capitalist society through the exercise of monopoly and politico-military power.

Now with the precious metals (specie) which they secured from the New World, the merchants were able to negotiate even better deals with their metropolitan royal patrons. They were also able to expand trade with the rich countries of the Far East, insofar as they could now trade this New World specie instead of the small range of inferior trade goods which backward Europe could offer for access to the cotton, silks, spices and ivory of the Far East.

The massive inflows of wealth from colonial exploitation, by historical irony, choked the capitalist development of Spain, the leading colonial power of the 15th and 16th centuries. On the one hand, it meant more wealth in the hands of the big merchants and, in this sense, the potential for large scale capitalist production was enhanced. On the other hand, gold and especially silver were so plentiful that the nobility of Spain could import all the luxuries they wished to have so that there was little incentive for merchants to organize production. The inflows of gold and silver generated an inflation in Spain, and subsequently the rest of Europe. This further redistributed wealth from the fixed income classes — landlords and peasants — to the merchants.

England was a relative late-comer in the scramble for colonies. This was partly due to its relative backwardness in shipping but mainly due to the fact of twenty years of civil war in which the monarch and his entourage lost power to the new revolting class of yeoman farmers. Well before the end of the Civil War, Cromwell's armies occupied Ireland, England's first colony of conquest, decimating its population and sharing out its land among the conquering Englishmen. It was likewise Cromwell who undertook the first naval expedition to drive the Dutch from the high seas and clear the way for the supremacy of English merchants in colonizing the four corners of the world.

The merchants, who previously had backed the kings of England, soon switched allegience to the victorious rising class forces of capitalist landowners and obtained such famous monopolies as the East India Company and the Royal West Africa Company and the Bank of England. The merchants now began to organize production. Profit-making required a steady supply of goods produced cheaply. Whereas the mediaeval merchant existed in the pores or interstices of social production, the new merchants sought to dominate the producer.

With the enclosure movement, England was turned into sheep runs and large capitalist farms producing commodities for sale via the merchants. Wool became England's principal domestic export and the great wool merchants dominated the trade. By the end of the 18th century the proletariat was an agricultural proletariat of farm hands; and the independent peasant had all but disappeared. These displaced peasants were absorbed in the *putting-out system* whereby men, women and children were cruelly exploited spinning and weaving wool cloth; and kept in perpetual debt to the merchants who supplied looms, materials, etc. and who, of course, kept the accounts. Outside the town limits, the guilds had no jurisdiction and goods could be made with different techniques or materials and the conditions for work cheapened.

The other form of production was the *manufactory*, a building in which several artisans were gathered to produce the same commodity. For example, several spinners might be brought together under one roof, where common supervision and raw material supply was possible. Manufactories were located in the towns and gave rise to increasing specialization and division of labour.

Capital thus began to take charge as it were of social production. That is, the merchants, not content with the available surplus production, began to organize production themselves. But it was merchant capital and the merchants' primary interest was in trade. In their mercantile conception of the accumulation of wealth, they naturally saw that the gain of the one was the loss of the other. Applied to international trade, where they were in a position to exercise monopoly control the merchants grew wealthy by buying cheap or securing goods by piracy and plunder and in turn selling dear. And, as well, England grew wealthy at the expense of its colonies. The big merchants secured trading monopolies by Royal Authority, so as to minimize the risks on their invested capital. Colonial economic policy was therefore a mere extension of this.

The merchants consolidated their economic dominance of the English economy in the revolution of 1640-80, when Parliament — then the mouthpiece of the bourgeoisie of capitalist landlords, large capitalist farmers and urban merchants — successfully won the right to make laws. This was the political basis for sweeping away the last vestiges of feudal privilege and mobilizing state power behind the interests of the merchants. With this newly won power, English merchants began to compete vigorously for colonies.

In 1494, the Pope had divided the Americas between Spain and Portugal. This was ignored by the English merchants. The power of the Catholic Church, after all, had been broken in England when Henry VIII seized the church lands — kept some for himself — and then distributed the balance among his favoured merchants. (His divorce and marriage was only the pretext for dispossessing the Pope and appropriating church revenue). The competition for colonies lay at the basis of the wars among the colonial powers in the 16th and 17th centuries.

Through colonialism, the emerging capitalist powers of Europe, imposed a peculiar international division of labour in which the people and natural resources of the colony were exploited for the benefit of their ruling capitalist classes. But the intermetropolitan rivalry superimposed a division of the colonial world into the respective empires, later called "spheres of influence". Thus, there were Spanish, Portuguese, Dutch, English and French colonialism through to the 19th century. Late in the 19th century there was to be American, Japanese, Italian, Belgian and German colonialism as well. This process of subjection and exploitation — colonialism — has left historical scars on almost every Third World country by way of political, economic and cultural ties with the "mother country".

2. Industrial Capitalism

The capitalist mode of production was not consolidated until the Industrial Revolution of the late 18th century. Many of the preconditions had been laid in the era of mercantilism. Capital had been accumulated through the expropriation of the landed nobility and the exploitation of colonial peoples. By being concentrated in fewer and fewer hands, the potential existed for capital — as wealth — to be transformed into machines, equipment, raw materials, buildings, and other means of production.

The accumulation process had also created a pool of cheap labour in the cities and even cheaper labour — slave labour or indentured labour — in the colonies. With nothing to sell but his capacity to labour, the English worker faced the alternative of capitalist exploitation or starvation. For the enslaved African in Jamaica, the choice was enslavement or freedom through active and passive resistance. Industrial capitalism expanded rapidly through the cruel exploitation of labour, enforced discipline of the work force, and increased specialization and division of labour.

Whereas under mercantilism, capital began "to penetrate production", under industrial capitalism, capital took full charge of production. The Industrial Revolution laid the technological basis for realizing the potential for capitalist production: that is, for bringing capital and labour together in the most modern production organization, the factory. The ability to harness and use steam power now made it possible to assemble large numbers of workers in one place. Sophisticated new iron and steel equipment and machines were built for mass production processes. With new sources of power, and the advantages of specialization of tasks in the factory's division of labour, labour productivity increased tremendously.

Vast new productive powers were released with this new organization of production. English factories poured out cheap manufactured goods, far in excess of the domestic market's capacity to purchase. After all, the domestic market was constrained by the low wages paid to the English worker. Furthermore, as capitalists reinvested their profits in new technologically advanced equipment, the productivity of labour continued to grow and the volume of goods in search of markets grew accordingly. This was a distinctive feature of this new mode of production: the ever increasing productivity of labour arising from the application of modern technology and scientific methods of production. The motive for this sprang from the characteristic behaviour of industrial capitalists: accumulation of capital through expanding production. That is, capital was constantly plowed back into production in order to reap more profits. This was possible, because more capital meant more workers; more workers, in turn, meant more labour to be exploited, or more unpaid surplus labour (in the form of surplus value) to be appropriated.

This was what made capitalism progressive in the 18th and 19th centuries. That is, in their drive for profits, capitalists were constantly revolutionizing the means of production and developing society's forces of production. But though capitalism flowered and developed, it brought extreme oppression and deprivation to the masses of people. Capitalism, after all, had developed from the ruins of feudalism. To the displaced peasantry, pushed off the land by the new capitalist farmers, only wage labour was offered either on the farm or mines or in sweatshops and factories in the cities where men, women and children toiled for 12-16 hours a day. Trade unions were strictly banned on penalty of deportation to Australia.

Every history of English capitalism records the widespread use of child labour, inhuman working hours and conditions, the squalor of workers' housing in industrial towns and cities, malnutrition, poor health care and banditry. In short, this was a condition of misery, with which Third World people today are well familiar. Of the treatment of English workers, a 'West Indian' slave-owning planter had this to say: "Most of all it was a society in which the abundance of goods produced by factories periodically exceeded the capacity of the masses to purchase them." To understand how in the midst of abundance and plenty, deprivation and want can run rampant is to know the essence of capitalism.

More than ever England needed her colonies as markets for cheap manufactures; but also as sources of supply of raw material and cheap consumer goods for the working people. The relatively advanced English merchant capitalists had anticipated the problem of supply by organizing slave plantation production in Jamaica and other colonies as far back as the late 17th century. (Notice, that while English production was being reorganized with capitalist relations of production — in particular the use of wage labour — colonial production was organized on the basis of slave labour.)

The technological revolution (the Industrial Revolution) had created the basis for capitalists to accumulate wealth through production rather than trade. But access, by the industrialists, to markets was restricted by the monopolistic privileges traditionally enjoyed by the merchants. These had been protected by a range of tariffs on foreign goods. This made raw materials and other inputs purchased by the industrialists for the factories more expensive. Sugar in particular from the English slave colonies was more expensive by the end of the 18th century, than beet sugar produced by capitalist farmers in Europe. Grain too was more expensive by virtue of a tax levied under the Corn Laws on foreign grain, particularly French, to protect inefficient English farmers.

The new industrial capitalists felt hemmed in by the restrictive practices of the mercantilists and demanded instead freedom from all restrictions on economic activity. *Laissez faire* (literally, Leave us alone, or free trade) was their rallying cry. In particular, they opposed the Corn Laws and other protective tariffs levied on foreign goods on the grounds that this made their wage-costs too high. Similarly, they fought for the abolition of the Sugar Duties Act, which protected English colonial sugar.

One of the weapons they used in their struggle against a regime of privilege and corruption which favoured the merchants and the capitalist landlords, was support for the struggle to abolish slavery. Slave plantations after all, were an important source of economic power for a large section of the merchants. Its profitability had been built on monopoly privileges and as slave production grew more inefficient, its profitability was guaranteed by prohibitive tariffs against its competitors. The effect of these tariffs, was to raise the cost of labour to the industrial capitalists as the prices of consumption goods, in particular sugar, for the workers were kept artificially high.

Thus, for their own interests — primarily to free the economy from monopoly and state interference — the industrial bourgeoisie threw its weight behind the anti-slavery struggle. Having been displaced as the ruling stratum of the English bourgeoisie, the merchants lost the right to trade in slaves in 1807 and the right to exploit them in English colonies in 1838. Slavery continued in Brazil and Cuba until 1888 and in the U.S.A. until 1865.

3. Monopoly Capitalism

The 19th century encompassed the glorious age of English capitalism (mid-1840's to 1873) when it grew to dominate the entire home market and much of the world as well. Europe and the U.S.A. were undergoing rapid industrialization and railroad construction. This required imports of all types — machines, raw materials and consumer goods — from England, the most advanced industrial country. To meet the demand, production from English factories and mills expanded several fold. Some key sectors such as iron and steel, shipping and chemicals were stimulated to develop and expand in this way. In the Communist Manifesto, Marx observed that societies which the bourgeoisie could not conquer by the gun (e.g. China, India) were subordinated with cheap manufactured goods.

But though English capitalism prospered, it underwent frequent crises which brought adversity to the working people. That is, capitalism grew by way of short lived booms and recessions. Political economists have located the underlying contradiction responsible for crisis in the tendency for capitalist production to exceed the purchasing power of the home market. In the periods of boom, the workers' wages were too low and therefore the domestic market was small. Thus the home market could not absorb all of the output at prices profitable to capitalists. Goods were in the warehouses and showcases, the people needed them, but could not afford them. In the periods of recession, the capitalist thought the same wages were too high to make investment profitable. To this day this contradiction is the economic root cause of crises in the advanced capitalist countries. In it is reflected the essence of the class struggle between capitalists and workers.

The glorious age of capitalism ended in 1870 in the most serious crisis of its relatively short history. As in previous crises, but more so now than before, smaller capitalists and their weaker companies faced bankruptcy and/or absorption by bigger capitalists and their stronger companies. A wave of mergers of companies in England — as well as in the USA and Germany — created giant monopolies like Standard Oil Company, United Fruit Company, Anaconda, Unilever and other names familiar to Third World peoples. These monopolies stretched their tentacles across several sectors of the domestic economy; at the same time they developed vertical linkages within some sectors. More important, they stretched their tentacles overseas, particularly into the colonial economies reserved for exploitation.

The growth of monopoly capitalism was facilitated by the banks. Within banking too, there had been merger and concentration, as small banks were absorbed by big banks. The banks had intimate knowledge of their clients' difficulties and financial power to effect take-over and merger. In return they secured positions of influence and power within the giant monopolies. This is why Lenin saw imperialism or monopoly capitalism, as the hegemony of finance capital over industrial capital. Industry was now subordinated to banking. As the industrialists had subordinated the merchants so too they were now being subordinated by the financiers. The source of wealth was still human labour. The source of surplus was still exploited labour. The distribution of this surplus was now in favour of financiers, who loaned funds to enterprises. With the increased concentration of capital larger enterprises could be established. But the accumulation of capital meant the simultaneous growth of the working class to man the new bigger factories.

Workers organized themselves in mutual aid societies — e.g. burial schemes, credit unions — and unions, to resist exploitation and to struggle for their rights. The English Chartist movement of 1846 was the precursor of the modern trade union movement. In 1848, a wave of insurrections in France and Germany threatened social revolution. In 1871, the workers of Paris formed themselves into a commune and tried to take control of their own destinies. The uprising was drowned in blood but it bore the seeds of a new society, a society which negated capitalist exploitation. In the 19th century the contradiction between capitalists and workers heightened. This was due partly to the increased numbers of the working class, brought into being by capital accumulation. It was also due to the heightened consciousness of workers of their collective class interests.

For the world economy, imperialism meant the export of capital, and in particular from the advanced countries to the backward countries of the world economy. Capital was exported in search of greater profits than could be obtained with the same investment at home. This was possible because workers in the colonies could be exploited more intensively — super-exploited. Rights and benefits won by years of struggle by the English working class, for example, did not apply to the colonized worker. Capital was exported for strategic reasons such as securing raw materials. Mineral companies, for example, bought up land reserves and mining rights to prevent competitors from getting access to new and cheaper sources of raw material.

Intense rivalry developed among the monopoly capitalists to secure control of raw material sources and markets for manufactured goods. Even more intense was the rivalry among capitalists of different nations. Overseas investment (capital exports) was only feasible if each capitalist had the support and protection of his government and state. For England, and some other European powers, the state had already been highly developed, administering a unified nation and many colonies as well. The state had long been in the service of capitalists, particularly in using its naval might to police English colonies and protect the investments of English capitalists. For other countries, like the USA and Germany, the state was mobilized by capitalists to seek colonial hegemony. Thus the USA wrenched Mexico, the Philippines, Cuba and Puerto Rico from Spain and landed troops to occupy Haiti. Germany formed a treaty with the rest of the European powers to complete the colonial partition of Africa by 1884. The World War of 1914-18 was a historical and logical outcome of rivalry among the imperialist powers.

Capitalism, after 1870, became monopoly capitalism. Now big monopoly capitalists and their giant corporations, especially banks, dominated the economic life of society.

Pushed into the background were the small industrialist and merchant. The modern multinational corporation began to dominate the world economy, and draw together workers from different countries in international production processes. The basis for this had been laid in the old colonial system which was refurbished and expanded. By 1884, all the non-white peoples of the world had been colonized to one degree or another.

In addition to the old forms of surplus extraction, the colonies now lost surplus through profit repatriation and debt payments. More than ever, the state was required to establish and preserve the conditions favourable to capitalist accumulation. This was the era of accumulation on a grand scale, on a world scale.

4. Capitalism, Colonialism and Imperialism

Modern colonialism must be seen as the mechanism by which the developing and expanding capitalist social system in Europe imposed a division of labour on the world. As capitalism developed through its three main stages, so too colonialism passed through three main stages.

Colonialism Stage I. In this stage the colonial surplus was conquest and plunder which corresponded to the early period of the mercantilist stage of capitalism. Spain and Portugal were the leading mercantilist powers then. For Jamaica, this was the period 1492-1655.

Colonialism Stage II. This was the period of direct investment by metropolitan capitalists in the colony. Foreign capital began to organize production at the ultimate expense of indigenous production. This period corresponded to late mercantilism and industrial capitalism. England was the leading capitalist power in this period. For Jamaica, this was the period of 1655-1838.

Colonialism Stage III. This is the age of imperialism. Metropolitan countries of Europe divided up Africa between them at the Berlin Conference in 1884. And the intensified struggle between them for resources and markets resulted in two World (Imperialist) Wars. England was the leading capitalist power until after the second Imperialist War when the United States of America became the top metropole. But Western Europe, especially Germany, and Japan presently threaten the hegemony of the United States.

In this stage, world capitalism came to be dominated by finance capital. And the monopoly control of production and international trade by multinational corporations lessened the need for maintaining colonies. Besides liberation struggles of colonized peoples throughout the Third World made it increasingly impossible to maintain the system of direct colonialism. Neo-colonialism is the order of the day. For Jamaica, this is the period 1865 to now.

Diagram 3.1 shows a model of the colonial system while Diagram 3.2 shows the phases of colonialism and the associated phases in the development of capitalism on a world scale.

MODEL OF A COLONIAL SYSTEM

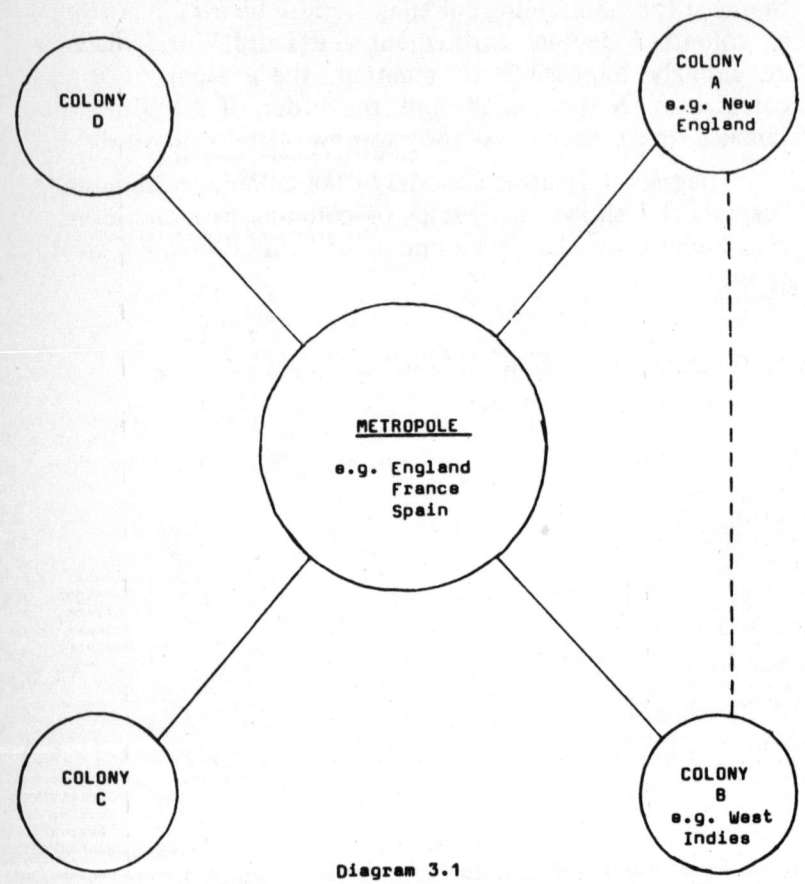

Diagram 3.1

Notes: (i) Broken lines indicate secondary/marginal trade either because (a) it was part of a triangular trade under metropolitan domination, or (b) it was illicit trade — smuggling.

(ii) In most cases there was little or no trade among colonies, because of their similar productive structures.

(iii) In Diagram 3.1, Colony A represents the "settler colonies" of New England (later, USA) whereas Colony B is a "colony of exploitation" (e.g. West Indies, Southern American Colonies. Colony A eventually becomes a new metropole in Phase II/III whereas Colony B remains a neo-colony.

THE PHASES OF COLONAILISM/CAPITALISM

Phase I : 1500 - 1650

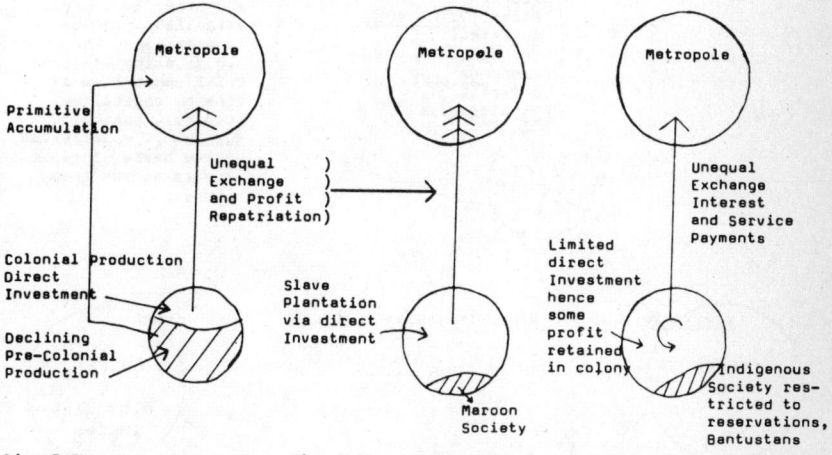

Primitive accumulation of capital by plundering natural wealth; e.g. gold, silver

Pre-colonial society, not yet re-organized by colonialism

Dia. 3.2a

Phase II : 1650 - 1870 — Mercantile Capitalism : 1648 - 1760
Industrial Capitalism : 1760 - 1870

Dia. 3.2b : The General Case

Dia. 3.2c : Caribbean, U.S. South, N.E. Brazil (Plantation America) ("Colonies of Exploitation")

Dia. 3.2d : New England, Australia ("Colonies of Settlement")

__Diagram 3.2__

/Diagram 3.2 (Cont.)

Phase III : 1870 - Present — Monopoly Capitalism, 1870-now

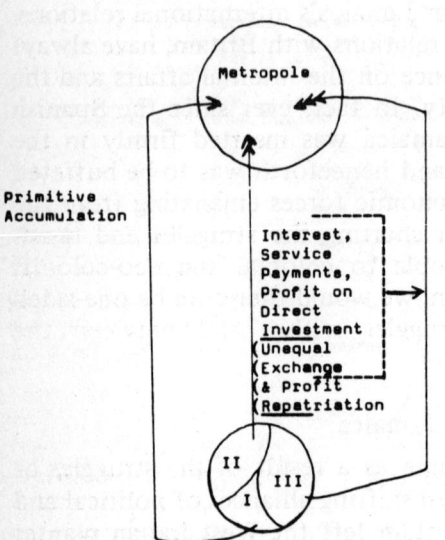

Notes

I   Vestigal pre-colonial pre-capitalist economy.

II   Direct investment in colonial production (e.g. slave plantation production established in Phase II: period of Mercantile Capitalism.

III   Modern Industrial/ Mining/Tourism/Banking and other services, established in age of imperialism - the sequestering of industrial capitalism by finance capitalism (monopoly capital). Surplus is repatriated on the basis of capital exports to the (neo) colony.

Dia. 3.2e : Modern Neo-Colonialism

CHAPTER 4

THE EMERGENCE OF THE PEASANTRY IN THE WOMB OF IMPERIALISM
From Emancipation to 1865

As we have seen so far, Jamaica's international relations, particularly the economic relations with Britain, have always exerted tremendous influence on the internal affairs and the development of the society. In fact, ever since the Spanish invasion and conquest, Jamaica was inserted firmly in the emerging world economy and henceforth was to be buffeted by powerful social and economic forces emanating from the big capitalist countries. In charting the struggles and resistance of the Jamaican people to colonial and neo-colonial oppression and exploitation, we would therefore be one-sided to neglect the class struggles within and between the advanced capitalist countries.

1. Birth of Capitalism in Jamaica

Emancipation had come as a result of the struggles of the slaves for freedom when shifting alliances of political and economic forces within Britain left the West Indian planter class too weak to defend its ownership of property and people. The slave plantation economy was now transformed into a capitalist plantation economy, but in a particularly distorted fashion. Most of the slaves who could do so fled the hateful estates and captured Crown Land in the mountainous interior, or bought available lands. But as well, many were forced by their economic circumstance to keep working for subsistence wages on the plantations.

The ex-slaves who could buy land had accumulated savings from their provision grounds during slavery. Recall that the slaves were granted small provision grounds to supplement the estate rations provided by the slave-master. The produce of these gardens were sold at regular Sunday markets and in some cases, slaves were able to put away a little savings. This Sunday Market was an important institution which acquired and enhanced economic importance for peasant struggles and transformation of the economy in the post-emancipation period.

In the first place, the Sunday Market was a meeting place for the slaves where information concerning the various local struggles and other important news was passed on. In addition, during the years of guerilla resistance, the Maroons were able to purchase supplies and later on to engage in regular trade. It was at the Sunday Market that the message of Christianity in all its forms was disseminated by missionaries. At the Sunday Market, christian missionaries found a captive audience whose circumstances made them receptive to the message of liberation through spiritual redemption. This was to become an important aspect of the outlook of the emerging peasantry. Finally, the Sunday Market was the fore-runner, in many cases geographically as well, of the system of parochial markets through which peasant produce is distributed throughout the island; and it laid the foundations for the relatively highly developed infrastructure of roads leading from the hilly farming districts into market towns. Thus, a basis was being laid for diversification of the economy from the mono-culture of King Sugar.

Emancipation gave rise to the peasantry and at the same time accentuated the demand for land to support their independent existence. Ownership of land remained monopolized by the British Crown and the planters. What lands the ex-slaves could capture or buy was marginal land, since the best land was reserved for sugar cane production. That is why even today, the fertile plains of the country are owned by large land-owners and are primarily used for sugar cane. At the same time, the peasantry has been forced to wrestle a subsistence standard of living from "rock-stone and hill-side", in many cases with his bare hands and machette.

While Emancipation meant that the white planters could no longer own African people as their slaves, they still owned the land and therefore held the key to the survival of the ex-slaves as free and independent producers. To ensure a supply of labour to the estates, every effort was made to prevent the ex-slaves from getting land. Two kinds of laws were enacted. One set restricted the sale of land to the ex-slaves, the other set were Vagrancy Laws which were used to victimize the landless. These laws, together with heavy land taxes, served to ensure a supply of labourers who had no choice but to work for cheap wages — penny a day — on the estates. Thus, some of the ex-slaves became wage labourers and the Jamaican proletariat was born. The Jamaican worker was now as free as any other proletarian. That is, he had long been freed of any ownership of land or any other means of production, from the days of slavery. But now that he owned himself he was free to starve, having no means of independent survival; or free to sell his labour power cheaply to the capitalist planter. That is to say, plantation capitalism deliberately created a surplus labour situation to keep wages at the minimum subsistence level of survival.

The old slave plantations had by Emancipation been experiencing steeply rising production costs on account of inefficiencies exacerbated by the struggles of the slaves. The number of estates had declined over the years, as the more inefficient ones fell into bankruptcy and ruinate. Those which could survive with a paid labour force became capitalist institutions proper in so far as production was carried on by wage labourers; in the language of our methodology, the characteristic social relation of sugar production was now the capital-labour relation.

Slave production had some features which facilitated the transformation to capitalist production. In the first place, this was large-scale production with the division of the labour process into simple tasks suitable for slave labour. Here large numbers of workers were assembled under a unified hierarchy of supervision. Output accrued to the planter — as owner not only of land and other physical means of production, but human/slave means of production as well — and was sold on the international capitalist market. It is here in particular that one sees the full meaning of Marx's observation that wage-labour was but "a veiled form of slavery". For what had really changed in the life of the ex-slave turned agro-proletariat?

While the sugar economy transformed and developed, there emerged alongside it a peasant economy. In effect, the latter was to become a reserve for the capitalist sugar economy. It was a reserve of labour available for peak demand at harvest and expansion. As a reserve army, it served to keep wages on the estate low since the planter could always obtain workers willing to accept what he offered. But it was also a reserve which supplied food and consumption goods (handicrafts) to the estate labour-force and thereby supplemented its meagre wage earnings. Thus, there remained strong family and economic relations between the agro-proletariat and the peasantry.

2. Peasant Struggle, State Repression and the Birth of Imperialism

The economy now had two aspects:[1] capitalist plantation sugar production for export and peasant subsistence production — but it was the capitalist aspect which dominated. Its dominance rested on the monopoly of the land, capital and other means of production. It was maintained by the force of the state with its pro-capitalist laws and militia. It was sanctioned and justified by the ideology of racism which led to attempts at the suppression of African cultural forms and values and the propagation of selected aspects of European (English) culture.

The Jamaican peasantry was born struggling for land. As the years passed the struggles intensified and had their first major climax in the rebellion led by Paul Bogle in 1865. Emancipation deprived the planters of their captive slave labour force. After the years of brutal exploitation on the estates the planters knew that provided the ex-slaves could obtain land, they would never return to the back-breaking estate work for low wages. They therefore sought to tie as many ex-slaves as possible to the estate and to encourage the immigration of indentured East Indian servants. Their key was the colonial state.

When Marx defined the state as an instrument of the ruling class he was never more correct than in the case of the Jamaican colonial state. Throughout the period of slavery the state's principal function was the repression of the slave and the maintenance of the slave society. It also had a token role of defending the colony against encroachment by England's rivals and enemies. The most important aspects of the state were the legal system and a militia/police force, the chief means of repressing the slave. The English Crown was represented by an English governor, who together with his personally appointed Privy Council exercised executive power.

---

[1] To some extent the Maroons had been engaging in peasant production. But this kind of production did not really become significant until the post-Emancipation period.

But there was also a legislative assembly which in reality served only in a consultative capacity to the governor. The assembly itself was totally dominated by the capitalist planters, as it was they alone who met the legal (property) requirements for holding a seat in the assembly. The law further restricted the franchise to vote to those who were propertied. Thus, though it pretended to be a popular institution through which the will of the people could be expressed, in reality it was only a forum for the mobilization and articulation of the planters' interests.

Throughout slavery there had been a fundamental unity of interests between the colonial executive (governor) and the legislative (the planters) in maintaining Africans in slavery. Nor, of course, did they disagree on the question of private ownership of the physical means of production — particularly land. Nevertheless, there had always been minor struggles between both branches of state, with the planters asserting themselves by refusing to approve the governor's budgetary proposals. The planters were forever agitating for more repressive laws to discourage the ex-slaves from squatting on land and for grants to import indentured servants.

Thus, by 1865, less than a generation after Emancipation, the vast majority of ex-slaves were still landless peasants, over-burdened with taxation on the goods they bought and on the land they cultivated. In St. Thomas, in that year, an incident was sparked off by the unjust treatment of a small free farmer accused of "squatting" on land he had already bought. Angered by this, some of his fellow farmers marched in protest under the leadership of Bogle demanding land, an end to oppressive taxation and called on the black people to rise up against the racist colonial oppression and to claim Jamaica which was rightfully theirs.

Simultaneously, a member of the mulatto middle class, George William Gordon, used his seat in the House of Assembly as well as public meetings to denounce the system. Gordon saw the misery of the people, particularly on the estates and raised his voice in protest against the repressive colonial regime of the day — that of Governor Eyre. He called upon the poor unemployed and downtrodden to unite in protest against the conditions imposed on them.

These two challenges to the colonial system coincided in time, became intertwined and came to be called "the Morant Bay Rebellion". Here, we see outlines of an important alliance: the peasantry, the agro-proletariat, and the mulatto middle class. Though in decay, the colonial government was nevertheless sufficiently strong to drown the uprising in blood; and for a time at any rate, the differences between the governor and the planters were put aside. For they saw the rebellion as a fundamental challenge to the rule of private property and the system of racial oppression in which it was instituted.

The political crisis brought a new constitution and a new governor. The "Crown Colony" colonial government took the opportunity to put the planters under manners as well and abolished the "representative (planters') assembly". With these, came new laws and a re-organized police force. The new laws victimized the peasantry by removing them from land that they had captured and then threatened them with fines and imprisonment for vagrancy. Thus, the fundamental oppressive role of the state was enhanced though in different forms.

3. Class Formation

The post-emancipation period is characterized by the development of the following class formation:

(1) *The emergence and growth of the Jamaican peasantry* — black African ex-slaves and their descendants.

(2) The rationalization and consolidation of the sugar export economy as pure capitalist production. Hence *there emerged an agro-proletariat* (an agricultural wage-earner) *with deep social, cultural and economic ties with the peasantry.* Indeed, many small peasants to this day are part-time peasant and part-time rural-proletariat. Indentured East Indians and African ex-slaves formed this class.

(3) The *growth of a mulatto middle class or petit-bourgeois of professionals, preachers and small proprietors* was also an important feature of the new society. They had sprung from the rape of the African women by the white slave master, and in a real way were the human product of the slave plantation society. It was frequently the case that paternity evoked a touch of benevolence from the slave

masters. In such cases, then, offsprings were given light tasks usually around the estate's Great House, given an education — sometimes in England — or granted small properties as a start in life. Nevertheless, many — no doubt the majority — were disowned and disenfranchised.

It is here that began the syndrome of disowning children born outside of marriage which torments the official self-perception of almost all bourgeois families. For the pattern of bourgeois men seducing their female employees — usually African, but East Indian women as well — has been carried on by the social and economic descendants of the old plantocracy. The hypocrisy of plantation-bourgeois society is never more sharply in relief than when the bourgeois officially disown their children, particularly where the ethnic mix is obvious. Even worse, behind the veil of official denial of paternity, some have secret contact with their 'own offspring'. This phenomenon is most evident among the bourgeoisie but manifests itself at all levels of the society though much less so among the lower peasantry and the working class. This is not surprising in that the mores, values and ideology of the bourgeoisie dominated the society and permeated all social classes; though the further down the social ladder the more these values and mores are transformed and distorted.

This mulatto middle class — originating out of the antagonistic racial and class contradictions of the society — was destined to play the role of buffer between the two great classes. Their social circumstances — principally professional and small propertied — permitted them the independence and illusion of security of small producers with their own means of production. Their petit-bourgeois social existence dictated a petit-bourgeois consciousness, with interests partly tied up with the capitalist planters and partly with the peasant and proletarian masses. And, of course, their racial origin and ascriptive features — colour, hair, speech, etc. — made them ideally suited as a buffer class between the white capitalists and the black working classes.

From the early beginnings of the peasantry the leading ideologues were the teachers and preachers. In many villages only the resident preacher or teacher — often the same person — was literate and therefore served as official interpreter of written news and official/legal documents. Because of its close relations with the peasantry and the agricultural workers on the sugar estates, the emergent petit-bourgeois understood the oppression, frustrations and aspirations of the masses. They shared them, too, for despite their relatively high status as "free coloureds" or "brown men", they were still second class citizens with a limited political franchise in a society still totally dominated by the capitalist planters. Thus, they, too, were oppressed and exploited through unequal trade by colonialism. They, too, were violated by the racist domination of European culture. And they responded in a range of forms of alienation, from apeing the ways and outlook of the colonial master to outright rejection.

But at the same time, compared with the masses of black working people, the mulatto middle class was extremely privileged. In this regime of private property no matter how barbarous its racist social forms, the petit-bourgeois had vested interests which brought a fundamental coincidence of interests with the capitalist planters and merchants. This ambiguity is the key to understanding the political role of the petit-bourgeois as a buffer in the struggles of the Jamaican people.

(4) *Then, there were the merchants.* They were all foreign. In the beginning, of course, there was only import/export trade — goods for the estate in exchange for sugar — monopolized by English merchants. Then came the itinerant traders who travelled through the countryside from estate-to-estate. Even today, itinerant traders hawk consumer goods on pay-day. There were the Jews and the Lebanese which the Jamaican people have collectively called Syrians. Much later came the Chinese. Some had come as early as the 1850's as part of the attempts to use indentured servants (quasi-slaves) after Emancipation to supply the estates with cheap labour. In some Caribbean countries, notably Trinidad and Guyana, thousands of Indians were brought in to man the estates. Both Indians and Chinese came to Jamaica in this way, though the Chinese were much fewer in number. It was more a second wave of migration of Chinese that came at the beginning of the 20th century as part of a large migration out of China primarily to South East Asia. They established a network of small grocery shops ("chiny shops") throughout the rural towns and villages catering primarily to the consumption needs of the peasantry. This strata of the merchants was closest to the masses in a number of important

respects which we will examine later.

Thus, all of the merchants were of minority ethnic origins. They came from trading backgrounds and were allowed to insert themselves in a special way in colonial Jamaica. They were "socially white"; standing above the black masses but nevertheless below the European plantocracy. Again, this reflected the relative social power of the classes in terms of their control over capital. It also suited the racist pattern of social stratification with the white people on top and the black people at the bottom. To be sure, these minorities were small and tended to be clannish and exclusive. Nevertheless, there were minor class/race contradictions among them particularly against the Chinese. These paled to insignificance compared to the collective hostility against the black masses, a contradiction based to be sure on the private ownership of the means of production by the planters and merchants but which manifested itself as racism against the African people.

(5) Finally, there was the *white European plantocracy*. They owned the capitalist plantations while their compatriots directed the colonial civil service and administered the state. Among the white planter class were those born on the plantations in Jamaica from expatriate British planter families. This category of *creole* Europeans became a powerful force in latter day Jamaican politics.

This, then, was the social structure as it emerged in the post-emancipation period. To complete the discussion, we must now analyse how the ruling plantocracy employed the colonial state to hold the class and race contradictions in check by repressing the popular struggles of the oppressed masses.

POST-EMANCIPATION SOCIAL STRUCTURE OF JAMAICA

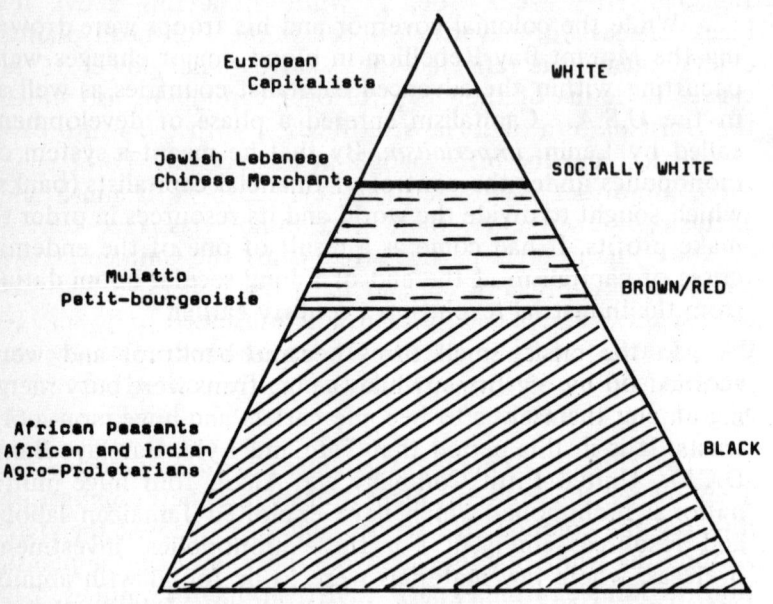

Diagram 4.1

CHAPTER 5

THE EMERGENCE OF THE WORKING CLASS:
From the Morant Bay Rebellion to 1938

While the colonial governor and his troops were drowning the Morant Bay Rebellion in blood, major changes were occurring within the advanced capitalist countries as well as in the U.S.A. Capitalism entered a phase of development called by Lenin, *imperialism*. By that he meant a system of monopolies under the control of financial capitalists (banks) which sought to divide the world and its resources in order to make profits. It had come as a result of one of the endemic crises of capitalism at the end of a long secular boom dating from the industrial revolution a century earlier.

In the crisis, small firms became bankrupt and were gobbled up by big firms; while the big firms were busy merging among themselves to become cartels and huge monopoly trusts. It is in this period that Tate and Lyle, Barclays Bank D.C.O., United Fruit Company and Alcoa, four huge multinational monopolies which have exploited Jamaican labour and resources emerged. For these monopolies, investment overseas, where raw materials were to be found with abundant cheap labour under the heel of colonial oppression, meant even greater profits than they could earn at home.

For many countries in the Third World, African countries in particular, this is the period when they entered the world economy. The Caribbean and Jamaica, in particular, were long accustomed to foreign investment – in plantations – by multinational capitalists. Nevertheless, the period was important for Jamaica too, for it marked the entry of American capital, then on the ascendancy and ultimately to eclipse Britain as the leader of the capitalist world. In particular, it saw the encouragement of peasant production of banana exports as well as the organization of production and marketing by the United Fruit Company. This was an important step linking the peasant economy to the world economy.

It was an important link for two other reasons. It brought the peasant the opportunity for migration which he took to Panama (Colon), Costa Rica and Cuba in the period around 1900 to the 1930's. Second, the banana boats brought the first tourists. By the turn of the century, the opportunities for making money in tourism began to be seized and a hotel building programme under Crown Colony government incentive was launched.

1. The Banana Trade

The impact of banana production is important for a number of reasons. First, it marked the second major wave of foreign investment into the economy, this time from the U.S.A.. This was the era of the United Fruit Company. Not only were facilities for shipping bananas developed — warehouses, purchasing stations, etc. — but many old sugar estates, some abandoned through bankruptcy, were purchased and put under bananas.

Initially, the black peasantry produced the fruit while mulatto merchants acted as buying agents for United Fruit Company; thus accumulating capital to become planters themselves. (White sugar planters ignored this at first as "backwoods nigger business". But the profitability of bananas and the declining demand for sugar later changed their attitude). This meant of course a new and vigorous boost for the continued monopolization of land by big capitalists and a further obstacle to the peasants' acquiring land. The new foreign capitalists and the mulatto merchant/banana planters thus objectively sided with the old plantocracy in the struggle with the peasants over land.

Second, banana production helped to diversify the economy while reinforcing its original export orientation. In the first place, the addition of another major export crop broadened the basis for export earnings. In the second place, incomes earned in banana production stimulated peasant production of domestic consumer goods — foodstuffs and handicrafts. For banana production, unlike sugar was amenable to small scale hill-side production, and required far less labour, while fitting in well to the mixed cropping regime of the subsistence-production oriented peasantry.

Many peasants with access to land seized the opportunity to earn cash, and in this way banana production injected a significant stream of cash into the peasant economy. Demand for local foodstuffs also expanded as workers on the banana plantations spent their wages on peasant output of foodstuffs. Thus the peasant economy was stimulated directly and indirectly by the banana trade.

At the same time, together with sugar, banana production for export dominated the economy as indicated by their command of land, human, and other physical resources. In this sense, the capitalist export sectors dominated the peasant sector, which was increasingly marginalized and made to function as its labour reserve. By the end of the 19th century export earnings from banana production significantly exceeded those of sugar. But the basic pattern of socio-economic relations and institutions had already been determined by sugar.

Third, with the banana trade came other new economic possibilities. There was a fledgling tourist trade which by the turn of the century was obtaining government assistance in the form of incentives for hotel construction. In addition, there were new vistas and possibilities for migration. The banana trade rested principally on the technological revolution in shipping, in particular faster ships with refrigeration facilities. This was part of a worldwide revolution in transport embracing the construction and opening of the Suez (1869) and Panama (1904) Canals. As it became very much cheaper to bring tropical produce to the fast growing markets of the industrial capitalist countries, there was a vast increase in cash crop and plantation cultivation in Asia, Africa, Central America and the Caribbean. For Jamaicans this presented opportunities for migration to Panama, Costa Rica and Cuba.

Finally, the banana trade stimulated important differentiation into rich, middle, poor, and destitute or landless strata. In general, it was the richer mulatto peasants with their larger land-holdings who profited from the banana trade and were able to accumulate a significant amount of wealth. In particular, many of the mulatto bourgeoisie were relatively big land owners — 100 acres — who seized and exploited the profitable opportunities of the banana trade by acting as brokers between the small peasants and the foreign imperialist marketing concern ("UNIFRUITICO"). For the collection agents earned profits by trading for small peasants and selling them supplies. Some of these brokers, dealers or agents later became full fledged merchants. Black produce dealers also came into the fore, trading in other lesser export commodities, like ginger, etc.

By the turn of the century, then, the peasantry had become stratified into a social pyramid with a broad base of poor and landless black peasants and with a narrow apex of relatively well-to-do mulatto peasants.

The growth of banana plantation production also accelerated the growth of the agro-proletariat, i.e. those who earned the bulk of their living by working for wages on the estates. In addition, the numbers of dock workers, transport workers, and clerical workers involved in the collection, purchase, and shipping of exports also grew. Moreover, there was a rapid growth of women employed in domestic services.

Thus the proletariat not only grew in numbers, but diversified — embracing workers on plantations, workers on the docks and in transportation, clerical workers and domestic workers. Nevertheless the working class retained deep organic ties with the peasantry, many of them being part-time peasants and part-time workers.

The post-emancipation developments changed the character of the peoples' struggles by broadening the social base. Their goals became more concretely formulated and clearly articulated. On the eve of Emancipation, the class alignments of the peoples' struggles were reflected in the opposition of the slaves — and their uncertain Maroon allies — to the planters, backed by the colonial State. When the colonial State shifted its support, the planters were forced to accept emancipation. State support shifted as the class character of the policy of the English government shifted in favour of the new industrial bourgeoisie in England and against the planters' allies — the merchants.

Twenty-seven (27) years later, scarcely a full generation from 1865, the class character of the peoples' struggles in Jamaica had changed. Opposing each other were the peasantry and elements of the mulatto petit-bourgeoisie on the one hand, and capitalist planters and the Colonial State on the other hand.

Not surprisingly, the goals of their struggles were then becoming progressively more concrete: from "freedom" in 1838 to Bogle's demand for "land and justice".

2. Forms of Resistance

But while Bogle's was the practical militant organized struggle against the Colonial oppressors, there were other responses to oppression. One was migration, made possible as a result of the growth of the world capitalist economy. Labour was needed to carry out such grandiose projects as the Panama Canal as well as to man the sugar and banana plantations and railroad construction throughout Central America and Cuba.

In the late 19th century, thousands of Jamaicans left for Panama to help dig the canal, and for Costa Rica to build the railroad. The original company which began the Panama Canal folded after a few years, and it was not until 1904 that the project was revived under the aegis of the U.S.A. Government. Again, Jamaican labour was recruited by Costa Rica to work on banana estates, and in 1918 Jamaicans left to cut cane and perform domestic service in Cuba. Of course there were many who returned, but there were also many who were stranded in foreign lands. When the project was halted or completed, the migrants found themselves in dire straits without money, and victims of local hostility. We are suggesting that, among other things, migration was an escape from the hopelessness of poverty in which the majority of people lived.

Migrants are always expected to "look back" to their social origins by extending their assistance to their less fortunate relatives at home. Jamaican migrants "looked back" by remitting some of their income home to help the family's consumption and to invest in land, housing, or some small business. At the same time, the promise of opportunity encouraged further migration, so long as outlets existed. These remittances have since been an important source of capital inflow, and in some years, the most important sources of private capital inflows.

Then there were religious responses to oppression. Under the onslaught of Christian missionary wisdom, many sought "other-worldly" solutions to their earthly problems of poverty and oppression. Christianity offered liberation through salvation. This tendency to seek a spiritual solution manifested itself most clearly in the period of the Great Revivals.

Finally, the ideological response to oppression was varied. Bogle's demand for land and justice, we have argued, represented the tendency of the most organized sections of the black peasantry. But there began to emerge around the turn of the century, the rudiments of a nationalism. The heightening of race consciousness led to the articulation of an international ideology anchored in the national experience. Simply put, the focus of this new ideology was the nation of black people, now seen in contradiction with white Europeans. One logical extension of this was repatriation of black people to the homeland, Africa, with its vast land resources and minerals. In the late 19th century, this ideological tendency was embryonic in the work of people like Robert Love. In the 20th century, through the work of Marcus Garvey, it was to become a major ideological theme in the peoples' struggles wherever African people are dispersed.

3. Shockwaves from Imperialist Crisis

In the first third of the 20th century profound changes in the international economy and the international balance of political forces sent shock waves into every society. The impact of these on each society varied with the sensitivity of the economy and society to the surrounding world. Where the economy was deeply integrated within the world capitalist economy, and politically dependent, as was Jamaica, the impact was far-reaching. For Jamaica, the most important developments were:-

    (a)   World War I
    (b)   Bolshevik Revolution in Russia
    (c)   The Great Depression
    (d)   Ethiopian resistance to Italian Fascist Aggression.

World War I

The name World War I is a misnomer, simply because the whole world was not in fact at war, though the political and economic impact of the war was world-wide. Rather, it is better named after what it was, the first Imperialist War, since in reality the hostilities revolved principally around the older imperialist powers — U.K., Germany, Austria-Hungary, France, Russia and Japan. In fact, it had its origin in rivalry amongst the imperial powers for economic colonies to secure resources and markets; in addition, there were ongoing struggles for political, military and economic influence. In this sense, it was a military manifestation of deeper economic contradictions and struggles among monopoly capitalists in the respective imperialist countries.

For the colony of Jamaica, it meant an increased demand for goods to supply the British Army. Sugar, in particular, enjoyed good markets as a result of the destruction of European beet sugar industry by the hostilities. Banana production was not so fortunate and entered a deep slump during the war years as a result of natural disasters — disease and hurricane — and a shortage of shipping on account of the hostilities. Following a long decline from Emancipation, sugar production eventually climbed back up by 1930, almost to the level of Emancipation, except for a few years of weak markets in the 1920's.

The war also demanded men to serve as soldiers in the British Army. Colonized man was recruited to defend the Mother Country in its hour of danger. Years of colonial ideological domination undoubtedly instilled a sense of loyalty to England in the minds of many people, and some probably took great pride in defending the British Empire. For others, it was an opportunity to escape the misery of their social circumstances for unknown adventure and opportunities abroad. But there was another category — those who saw, in however incoherent a fashion, the possibility of meaningful reward for black people at the end of the war. Specifically, these black soldiers fixed their eyes on at least a portion of the German colonies in Africa as a reward for their services to Britain and her European Allies.

As it was, they were disappointed as the imperialist powers never seriously considered any such arrangement. The anger, disappointment, and frustration of the Black Veterans of all the imperialist armies — American, British, French — was to be one of the more militant threads of revolt woven together in the Garvey Movement.

The First Socialist Revolution (Bolshevik)

If the war was a response to imminent crisis in the world capitalist economy, it also shook the imperialist system sufficiently violently to create the political space for the first socialist revolution. The conditions for social revolution in Tsarist Russia had matured during the opening years of the war. By 1917 Lenin and the Bolsheviks had adopted the position of "Revolutionary Defeatism". By this they meant that working people had no business in any imperialist war, and should seize the opportunity to make revolution by overthrowing the pro-imperialist Tsarist government. In October of that year, the world's first socialist state was born. Henceforth, the balance of international political forces shifted increasingly in favour of the struggles of the oppressed peoples of the world.

Of course, news of the victory of the Bolsheviks must have encouraged the struggling Jamaican people. But under the yoke of colonial oppression, the revolution was maligned and distorted by British and American propaganda. It was not until the 1930's and 1940's that Jamaican revolutionaries began to study and organize for the propagation of socialist ideas arising out of the revolutionary experience of the USSR.

The Great Depression

War stimulates a capitalist economy, so long as its principal trading links remain intact, and so long as the war is fought in another country. On the other hand, where a country's trade is disrupted by naval blockade and it is the victim of invasion, its productive base and hence its economy is disrupted and sometimes destroyed. War dictates military expenditures which create demand for the necessary goods — especially weapons, food, transport, medicine. In this sense, war is good for capitalism, especially when it is faced with a crisis of stagnation or recession because of insufficient demand for the output of the economy.

The U.S.A. emerged as the leading capitalist power in the aftermath of the first Imperialist War. Already, at the turn of the century, there had been a considerable shift in Jamaica's trade to the U.S.A., with over a third of imports coming from the U.S.A. Supplying its allies, and even financing some of their needs, kept the U.S.A. economy vibrant and growing. The resumption in world trade after the end of World War I was short-lived. Within a decade, the U.S.A. economy plunged into a depression and triggered the worst crisis in the world capitalist economy to date.

In order to minimize the shocks to their economies, country after country erected protective barriers and world trade collapsed. Despite this, demand for Jamaican sugar and banana remained strong. Sugar production continued its slow recovery to the level of Emancipation. Banana production too recovered quickly from its problems during the war years, and by 1927 had surpassed all previous levels.

However, imports of consumer goods probably fell, thereby permitting some domestic production of substitutes.

Prior to 1930 however, manufacturing was quite insignificant, being confined primarily to sugar and rum manufacturing, some processing of agricultural crops — logwood, coconut, coffee, etc., as well as soft drinks and tobacco. On the other hand, there was a thriving handicraft production, though estate demand for the services of artisans declined with plantation production. With the cut-back in consumer imports, the people had to turn to native industry and handicrafts.

In Defense of Ethiopia

Finally, Ethiopian resistance to Italian aggression in the 1930's inspired black people all over the world and particularly in Jamaica. The newly crowned Emperor Haile Selassie I took on a role of Liberator/Messiah for a small section of the black peasantry. Selassie was acclaimed JAH by the Rastafari, an indigenous social movement which emerged from the intertwining of the black nationalism of Bedward and Garvey with the Africanized Christianity of the peasantry. In this period Rastafari was a politically insignificant sect, though the Governor and St. Thomas planters and the Gleaner expressed concern. However, forty years later it was to become so important that the major political parties would openly court the support of the Rastafari. The first PNP government of Norman Manley had to give the movement legitimacy on account of its strong social base, and since then Rastafari has become part of the body politics of Jamaica's two-party Westminster system.

4. A Hundred Years of Struggle — 1838-1938

One hundred years after Emancipation, a peasant economy established itself side-by-side with the former slave plantations, some of which were now producing bananas as well as sugar. In 1865, twenty-seven years after Emancipation, the peasantry made a decisive entry into Jamaican history and politics, into the class struggle. By 1938, seventy-three years later, it had consolidated itself *as a class* in the land struggles and in developing infrastructure to support the peasant economy — roads, markets, etc., which the State neglected.

For a minority of middling and rich peasants, cultivating bananas for export brought a reasonable (and sometimes a comfortable) standard of living. But the masses of the poor and landless lived a marginal existence, barely above subsistence level. The peasantry had grown and become differentiated into several strata: rich/upper, middle, poor/landless. Gisela Eisner estimated that there were about 184,000 peasants cultivating less than 50 acres in 1930. Her data also show that export production assumed increasing importance in peasant production until it reached 29 per cent in 1930, and that by then, 41 per cent of all exports originated from the peasants' production.

By the eve of 1938, the mulatto petit-bourgeoisie had also grown. Some fared well in agriculture, but most took to professions, shop-keeping, and public service in the State. Though materially far better off than the poor peasants, they were nevertheless politically oppressed like the peasantry under a constitution that limited the electoral franchise to men of substantial property.

For the peoples' struggles, 1938 was most important because it marked the revolutionary entry of the working class into Jamaican history and politics, into the class struggle. The working class spearheaded the revolutionary upsurge against the oligarchy and the colonial state in protest against low wages, poor working conditions and oppressive social conditions in general. To be sure, it was numerically small — only about 50,000 were urban — and still tied in many ways to the peasantry. It was primarily an agro-proletariat, although an increasing number were service workers, particularly female domestic servants. Prior to 1930, manufacturing, and hence the industrial proletariat was virtually insignificant. Yet, it was not sufficiently distinct from the peasantry as a class to form its own organizations (unions), to formulate its own goals: work for the unemployed, better wages for the employed; and to initiate militant political action against the colonial ruling class.

Although the working class took the initiative in 1938, with the support of the peasantry, leadership quickly passed into the hands of the mulatto petit-bourgeoisie. This class was, to the colonial authorities, more reasonable, far less radical, and more equipped to assume a share of national political responsibility and power than the angry black masses. Whereas the latter, if allowed, seemed intent on sweeping away the entire apparatus of social oppression, the mulatto petit-bourgeoisie had vested interests in the *status quo;* and that accounted for their political ambiguity. To be sure they demanded political rights for everybody, but their real interests were in securing a share of political power for themselves. At the same time, they shared with the ruling class the fear of total and complete destruction of the social order, in which they too had an important stake.

SCHEMATIC REPRESENTATION OF THE DEVELOPMENT OF CLASS STRUGGLE IN POST-EMANCIPATION JAMAICA

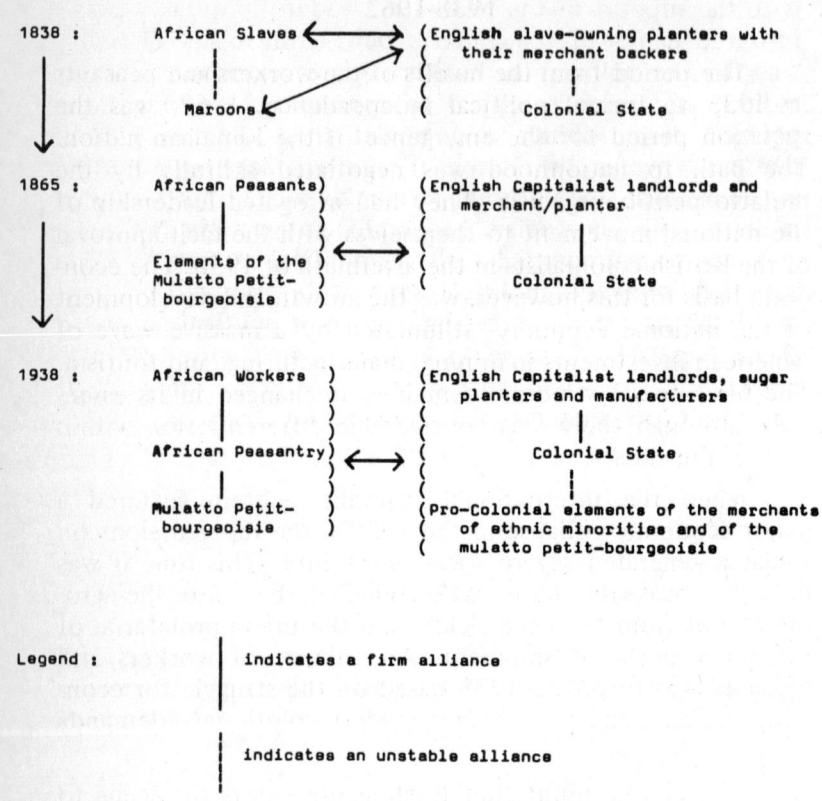

Diagram 5.1

CHAPTER 6

BIRTH AND GROWTH OF THE NATIONAL ECONOMY: 1938-1962

The period from the revolts of the workers and peasants in 1938 to formal political independence, 1962, was the gestation period for the emergence of the Jamaican nation. The path to nationhood was negotiated skilfully by the mulatto petit-bourgeoisie. They had arrogated leadership of the national movement to themselves with the tacit approval of the British colonialists in the aftermath of 1938. The economic basis for this however, was the growth and development of the national economy, stimulated by a massive wave of American investments in mining, manufacturing, and tourism. The basic social structure remained unchanged in its essentials, although there was considerable differentiation within each of the classes.

When the international capitalist system suffered a major economic collapse in the 1930's, the repercussions on Jamaica generated severe social instability. This time it was not the peasants alone who rebelled, but also the agro-proletariat from the cane fields, and the urban proletariat of the main ports of shipment. An alliance of workers and peasants was forged in 1938 based on the struggle for economic survival; and this alliance made revolutionary demands for some change.

It is at this point that Bustamante enters the scene to become a self-proclaimed leader of the dispossessed workers and peasants. The rebellion of 1938 linked the banana workers of Portland and St. Mary, the sugar workers of Westmoreland, St. Thomas and Clarendon, the dock workers of Kingston, Port Antonio and Oracabessa, to form a revolutionary brigade demanding social change. British troops once again quelled the rebellion as they did in 1865. But this time the leadership was not hanged.

Instead the colonial office accepted the leadership of Bustamante and Norman Manley in order to support the dominance of the mulatto petit-bourgeoisie in the emerging national anti-colonial movement. This class had always been the social buffer between the masses of the black people and the white European ruling classes. Now it was to be the political buffer and broker between the two great antagonistic classes — capitalists and workers. At the same time the colonial authorities managed to create a "divide and rule" situation, by establishing both Bustamante and Manley as rival political leaders, both having acceptable class backgrounds.

This rivalry was rooted in different sections of the mulatto and peasant petit-bourgeois. It was personified in the rivalry between the two leaders. It was institutionalized in a two-party competitive system of Westminster politics. But before proceeding to examine the politics of change, it is necessary to note carefully the official responses to the 1938 rebellion. The Crown detained one of the leaders, Mr. Bustamante, and neutralised the anti-colonial struggle by the manipulation of the two leaders.

The events of 1938 induced an official reaction in the form of establishing a Royal Commission to enquire into the social conditions of the British West Indies. That Commission was led by Lord Moyne and the report was published in 1945, the year after the war. The single most important recommendation of the Moyne Commission was to reiterate the recommendation of the 1897 Commission for the creation of a landed peasantry, thus giving the on-going land settlement schemes an extra shot in the arm ("an accelerated land settlement programme"). The other major recommendation of the Moyne Commission was that efforts should be immediately set in train to establish real representative self-government under a new system of Adult Suffrage. And so Jamaica got its new Constitution in 1944 which ended the period of rule by Crown Colony government.

1. The Political Party Struggle

It is important for us to examine the character, however briefly, of the two parties that eventually emerged under the new Constitution. The People's National Party was the first one founded in 1938, with the Bustamante Industrial Trade Union (BITU) as its worker-based institution. The ideology of the PNP was then Fabian Socialist, but it also accommodated some Marxian socialists who became the hardest working section of the Party, organising allied trade unions after the break-away of the BITU and the formation of the

Jamaica Labour Party. (The Busta/Manley split).

The Jamaica Labour Party (JLP) had a conservative capitalist ideology, and it sought in the words of its leaders, to provide only a little more bread and a little more butter for the working class and the peasantry. These limited objectives managed to appeal to the new electorate, which in 1944, voted the JLP into office. Within the People's National Party (PNP), their loss at the polls again in 1949 led to a reassessment of the possibility of retaining its Marxian components under the Party's rhetorical claims to Fabian Socialism.

In spite of the labour-supported strength of the Marxist element, the reactionary capitalist wing, led by Isaacs and Glasspole, managed to convince the Party Leader that the Marxists posed a threat to his authority and governance. Accordingly, the Marxist wing was eradicated with the expulsion of the 4H's (Ken Hill, Frank Hill, Richard Hart and Arthur Henry) in 1952 at the height of the Korean socialist struggle against international capitalism. And in spite of the impact of the Chinese revolution in 1949 and the establishment of the Vietnam Socialist state in 1946, the PNP Fabian Socialists carried out a McCarthyite campaign against revolutionary socialists and communists. After this point in the struggle, the People's National Party, like the JLP, articulated a liberal conservative ideology. PNP and JLP thereafter became like fish and fowl — there was none to choose. Both were capitalist parties, with one being a little more liberal than the other, depending on which one was in power at any given time.

We shall demonstrate this assertion by examining the economic policies of both party-governments in the post-war period. The economic policy pursued by all Jamaican governments since 1944 was a policy of dependence on international capitalism, by creating "a welcoming society" for foreign capital under the general rubric of "industrialisation by invitation".

2. Black Dispossession and Affirmation

With the new Constitution of 1944, the political scene in Jamaica evolved through various stages of self-rule until the country secured its constitutional independence in 1962. Much of official policy after 1944 came to be formulated by the new representative parliamentary system. There were two basic sources which guided policy formation. The Moyne Commission report was one of these, which contributed to the acceleration of land settlements as a means of easing land hunger.

But the type of land which eventually passed to the hands of the peasantry in this way was, in general, land of poorer quality than that held by the plantations, in sugar and other crops. The resulting peasant sector managed to secure minute parcels of land which were not of a sufficient size to generate even subsistence levels of income, because of the small size and the poor quality of the land involved. The basic contradictions between peasant and plantation and between workers and capitalists deepened over the period.

The limited inroads on the land question coming out of black people's struggle and the Moyne recommendations were to a large extent reversed with the appearance of bauxite and tourism, both of which served to alienate large acreages of land from the peasantry, thereby heightening the existence of land hunger. The black peasantry which was displaced by the inroads of bauxite and tourism migrated to the Kingston Metropolitan Area internally, and to England externally. And so, migration returns to the scene as it did in the late nineteenth and early twentieth centuries, as an escape from the dispossession and alienation generated by these forms of foreign capitalist penetration of the economy.

The second source that informed official policy was the Fomento Programme in Puerto Rico which gained the nickname "Operation Bootstrap". At the root of this policy is the provision of incentives to attract foreign capitalists to come and establish manufacturing activities. This programme of industrialisation by invitation led to the emergence of branch-plant capitalism, which in fact, never manufactured anything but was engaged in the assembly of components into finished products. From poultry meats in the agricultural sector to tyre manufacture in the industrial sector, the economic activity carried out was essentially one of a screwdriver type of production. The capital-intensive nature of many of these operations meant that no large number of workers would be employed, while the government forfeited the customs and income taxes which would have been secured without Incentive Legislation. Tax-free holidays, duty-free imports of raw materials, accelerated depreciation allowances, site rental in industrial estates, all cost the public sector a substantial amount of potential revenue. In return for this, the number of workers employed by the manufacturing sector under the Incentive Programme over a ten-year period was less than the growth of the labour force in a single year.

This "Puerto Rican model" of development was pursued vigorously by the first PNP government of 1955 to 1962 and by the JLP government of 1962 to 1972. In 1974, the People's National Party adopted an ideological commitment to the creation of a democratic socialist Jamaica and the policies since then have been moving in this direction, however slowly and haltingly.

3. The Second Coming of American Capital

The U.S.A. economy — and indeed most of the European capitalist economies as well — did not really recover from the Great Depression of the 1930's until they were stimulated by government expenditures on war preparations on the eve of the second imperialist war — World War II. The war of course prevented the recovery of world trade as commercial ships were mobilized for the war effort and those that were not were easy victims of warships.

The Jamaican economy, dependent as it was on world trade, continued to languish throughout the war. Economic conditions deteriorated even further and the misery of the people rose just as sharply. One positive effect, however marginal in significance, was the emergence of local manufacturing of consumer goods to replace unavailable imports. These goods were processed from locally-produced agricultural raw materials and thus an organic link was forged between the two sectors. Coconuts, for example, were used to make soap, cooking oil as well as other things. Cassava flour was produced to replace scarce wheat flour, and so on.

The scarcity of imports also helped reorient people's tastes to local foods and other kinds of goods. At the very least it taught them to live without many things which were felt to be necessary in normal times. There was less money in people's pockets because of the hard times, but a greater share of it now went to buy locally produced goods. As before, in periods of crisis when export production declined, production for the local market, utilizing local skills and raw materials, increased. The outlines of a national economy were becoming visible by the end of the war.

American capital had initially flowed in to set-up the banana industry in the late 19th and early 20th centuries. The second wave of American capital inflows came after the second imperialist war to mine bauxite and expand tourism. Demand for aluminium had been stimulated by the Korean War and the space exploration programme. Apart from the Americans, the Canadians (Alcan) came as well in search of bauxite and profits. Official government policy encouraged and welcomed foreign capital. Massive inflows of foreign capital also led to the establishment of "modern" branch-plant manufacturing and the expansion of the tourist industry. And, of course, their bankers came with them — First National City Bank, First Chicago, and Citizens. The Canadian and British banks were here long ago — Barclays, Bank of Nova Scotia, Royal Bank of Canada, while BOLAM emerged as a joint U.K.–Canadian bank.

Foreign capital financed and provided the technology for a tremendous diversification of the economy. But it was a peculiar diversification, in which the new sectors had no links among themselves and developed very few links with agriculture. Construction activity was the only domestic industry to derive any stimulus for growth from these new industries. Even that, of course, was limited and benefited as well from foreign capital, technology and expertise.

Despite this diversification, the post-war developments reinforced the basic import-export orientation of the economy. Almost all of the inputs, raw materials, services and even the skilled manpower were imported by the mining, manufacturing and tourist industries.. All of the bauxite and alumina and much of the manufacturing output was exported. All the tourists were North Americans. Further the exposure to North Americans and their higher standards of living whetted the appetites of the Jamaican people for the higher standard of living and the goods that went with it. Of course, few could afford it; for the masses without means, there were only hopes and dreams.

Thus the new sectors were primarily foreign owned, although more and more elements of the Jamaican bourgeoisie were taken in as partners, to front for the foreigners. The new investments created profitable opportunities for the Jamaican bourgeoisie as well. Merchants traded larger volumes of consumer goods as well as raw materials for industry. Some merchants also became manufacturers, producing goods — clothes, for example — that were formerly imported. Speculators got rich through real estate dealings, particularly the subdivision of residential land. Entrepreneurs of all sorts emerged selling services — entertainment, restaurants, transport. In short, a close relationship developed between the foreign capitalists and the local capitalists who depended on them for finance, technology, supplies and marketing. It was a client relationship, and as such justifies us calling the Jamaican bourgeoisie a *client* (or comprador) bourgeoisie.

4. Impact on the Social Structure

This client relationship made the local capitalists hardly more than agents in the foreign exploitation of Jamaican workers and consumers. The exploitative social structure, the bequest of centuries of English colonialism, facilitated the production and repatriation of economic surpluses by the new capitalists. The social relations of race/class were reinforced and institutionalized in the foreign establishments. At the top were the white expatriate or "socially white" (Jew, Lebanese, Jamaica white) Jamaican managers. Immediately below were the mulatto/brown, Chinese and Indian professionals, middle managers and clerks. At the bottom were the black workers.

The growth of the economy as we have seen provided profitable investment opportunities for services, particularly professional services. Elements of the brown middle class — the mulatto petit-bourgeoisie — seized these opportunities for social advancement and accumulation of wealth where, because of their property and/or education — in addition to their colour — they were able to do so. Furthermore, as decolonization proceeded, many British expatriate functionaries in the Civil Service, the schools and other public institutions returned home leaving their posts to Jamaicans. As the state bureaucracy grew, new jobs were created as well. Again it was the brown middle class which occupied the senior posts of management and administration, while the lower clerical, technical and menial services were left for the black workers. Thus middle order leadership in the economy — management, administration, technical experts — began to pass to the mulatto petit-bourgeoisie. At the top were the white expatriates, their white Jamaican partners and those they chose to regard as socially white — Jews, Lebanese, Chinese and some of the Indians.

There was also a tremendous expansion of the working class, recruited from the displaced peasantry and the lower strata of the mulatto petit-bourgeoisie who were unable to maintain their economic independence. With growth came differentiation into several strata. At the top of the working class were the highly skilled workers particularly in bauxite and alumina production. They earned high salaries — many times more than the Jamaican average — by Jamaican standards but lower than their counterparts in North America. Beneath this labour aristocracy, was a mass of low-skilled and unskilled labour manning the machines in the "sweatshop" factories, serving the guests in hotels, serving as domestic helpers for middle class and bourgeois homes, performing simple clerical and casual tasks for the state and working in service industries such as gas stations, transport and so on. Thus though the agricultural labourer was still at the bottom of the social pyramid he was joined there by a range of menial and casual workers performing one kind of service or another. The working class now assumed a new character; urban, industrial and service workers soon outnumbered the agricultural workers. The ties to the peasantry were weakened but nevertheless still remained intact.

Perhaps the greatest pressure has been felt by the peasantry: pressure from plantations, from mining, and from tourism, all competing with the poor peasant for the limited land base that Jamaica possesses. Naturally, the peasant fared worse in this competition. Peasants only managed to maintain a subsistence level when competition was not intense and when new income opportunities arose.

The effect of the relative decline of the peasantry has had far reaching effects on the Jamaican economy. Peasants are the main source of domestic food supplies and the relative slow growth of food supplies associated with the demise of the peasantry has contributed to increased food imports and rising food prices. This problem has been further aggravated in the past few years with the world capitalist shortage of food and animal feed. Food prices have risen faster than any other set of prices in the consumer price index. The resulting inflationary situation has had serious repercussions, both social and economic. On the whole, the real income of working class people has declined over the past few years. Food shortages are so acute in Jamaica at this time that systems of informal rationing, hoarding and black markets have developed.

Food shortages also have serious effects on the nutritional status of large groups of people. Jamaica is already characterised by serious nutritional imbalances for certain groups of people. Malnutrition is common among infants, especially pre-schoolers. One recent survey in Jamaica, for example, indicated that below one year of age, over ninety percent of infants receive less than the calorie intake recommended by FAO, and over eighty percent receive less than the recommended protein intake. (J.C. Waterlow, "Observations on Nutritional Conditions in Jamaica", CFNI, UWI, 1973). More general evidence shows that severe infantile malnutrition is common in hospitals; that there is a high death rate in children under four years; that most school children are under-weight and small for their age and that low intakes of both protein and calories are common among children and adults of low income groups.

The deteriorating economic situation of peasants and rural proletariat was instrumental in promoting rapid rates of rural-urban migration and of external migration. Peasants contributed significantly to the massive wave of external migration during the 1950's. Sale of land provided the wherewithal for some to go abroad. The economic circumstances of the rural· proletariat and the landless peasants prevented external migration, so that they contributed chiefly to the wave of internal migration to towns and cities. But the pace of urban industrial advance was not sufficient to accommodate them and they lacked the skills required in any case. And so, the growth of urban slums, of petty thefts, of prostitution, and other social ills are associated with that change.

Changes in the economic circumstances of the peasants reverberate on other sectors of the economy. The marketing of peasant output is carried on by petty traders who are referred to as higglers. These are usually women who purchase from farmers and retail to consumers in a network of public markets. Peasants purchase consumer and farming goods after selling their products in this network of market centres. But the prices received by peasants have not kept pace with the rise in prices for peasant inputs. Overall, the new modernising sectors of the Jamaican economy (bauxite, tourism, branch-plant manufactures) advanced at the expense of peasants and consumers.

Race and class remained joined, but with increased social differentiation, they began to loosen their hold on each other. More and more black people achieved middle class status, frequently through education and an undaunting will for social advancement. The civil service, in particular, was opened up to accommodate black senior administrators and managers. Most important, many black people acquired status through politics and (too often through politics), the material basis for maintaining that status. But in this period, the social mobility of the majority of black workers, and small peasants, and their children, remained the exception rather than the rule.

Similarly, some of the brown petit-bourgeoisie, were unable to maintain their independence and became wage earners. The lower sections of this class therefore became absorbed within the working class, more often than not, within the labour aristocracy. Within the ethnic minorities, the social differentiation expressed itself despite traditional co-operation within the minority group. Thus some Chinese prospered more than others, and some Lebanese capitalists absorbed others. There had always been deep cleavages within the Indian community, but now differentiation occurred within the lower strata. This phenomenon was evident in cane farming areas where Indian peasants were able to accumulate enough to go into trucking as private contractors.

Like the other ethnic minorities, their children were relatively well educated and moved into the ranks of the petit-bourgeoisie as professionals, technicians and managers. Still others established businesses of their own.

PRESENT PATTERN OF SOCIAL STRATIFICATION

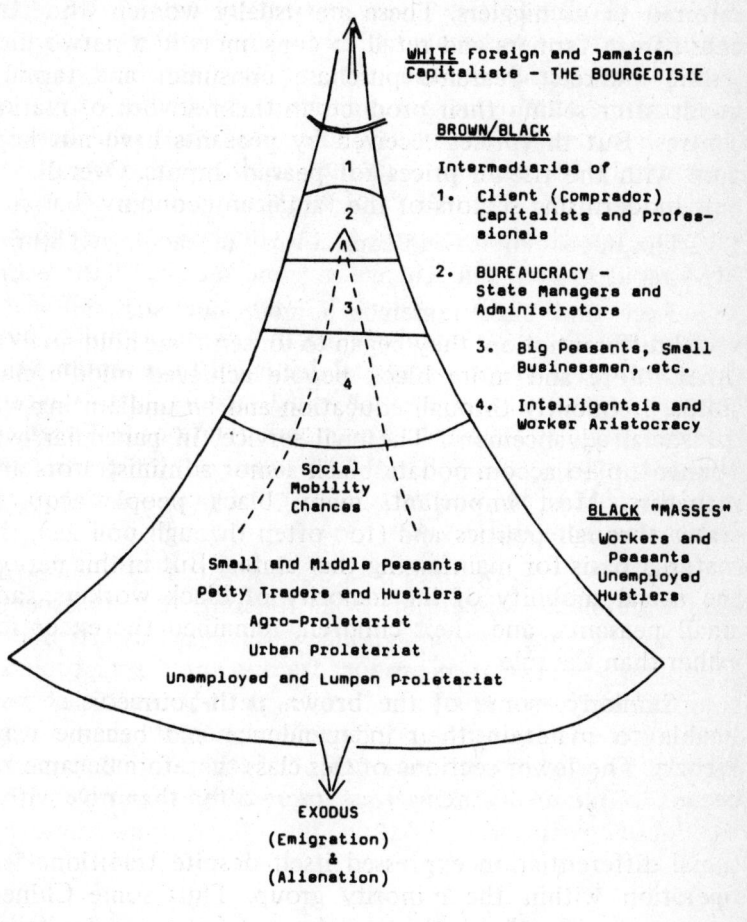

Diagram 6.1

The 50's in particular, were years of record economic growth. The benefits of that growth were unequally distributed, as dictated by the underlying unequal distribution of property. To the foreign investors went the lion's share of the profits. The rest was shared with the local bourgeoisie, a high salaried managerial elite and corrupt politicians. For the masses of people employment was rationed, wages were low, job tenure insecure, in addition to the unsatisfied land hunger. Accordingly the gap between the standards of living of the ruling classes and the masses of working people grew wider.

The impact of foreign capital was far-reaching. It stimulated rapid growth and change in some sectors of the economy even as it stifled others. It strengthened the hold of foreign capital, and particularly North American capital, over the resources of the country and deepened the economic ties between Jamaica and the advanced economies of North America. By 1962, Jamaica's economic relations had been re-oriented toward the U.S.A.; 39 percent of trade was now with the U.S.A. and the vast majority of post-war capital inflows were from the U.S.A.

By 1962, the outlines of a quasi-modern national economy were clearly discernible in all its contradictory aspects. As a result of the economic policies, this was a disarticulated economy, which in turn produced a disjointed society and a comprador polity. The path that led it there was to be pursued for the first decade after independence. By then contradictions in this kind of development of the national economy began to manifest themselves in socially explosive ways.

CHAPTER 7

POLITICAL INDEPENDENCE AND NEO-COLONIALISM
1962—1974

The process of constitutional decolonization was formally completed with political independence in 1962. The new political leadership had been groomed over the previous twenty-five years to administer the affairs of State. This meant presiding over a colonial bureaucracy, enforcing colonial laws and ensuring conditions for continued development of the economy along the lines initiated in the 1950's. To be sure the politicians spoke of nation building. But instead of a concrete programme of national construction all they offered were the symbols — flag, anthem, new stamps, new coins and the other paraphernalia of national symbolism.

The people chose Bustamante and the JLP to lead them into independence, and re-elected them five years later. In all they charted the nation for the first ten years of its path to independence. After the initial uncertainties surrounding the transfer of political power in 1962, foreign capital again flowed in to expand bauxite/alumina production, manufacturing, tourism and banking. More incentives were offered under an expanded programme of industrialization by invitation. Tight reins were held on working class militancy to maintain the atmosphere of industrial peace and low wages which attracted foreign investors. "We are with the West", proclaimed Bustamante.

A significant development in this period is the mushrooming of all sections of the client bourgeoisie and the middle classes. With the aid of the foreign banks and producing under licence and technology agreements with overseas parent companies, the Jamaican merchant-turned-manufacturer grew and prospered. So did the middle classes as high income jobs were created in the private as well as the State sector as a direct consequence of the increased purchasing power and increased economic activity resulting from the large volume of foreign investment inflows, particularly in the bauxite-alumina industry.

For the masses, matters were far different. The traditional emigration outlet to Britain had been closed. Now the only escape from rural landlessness was migration to the city, only to find urban unemployment. By the end of the first decade of independence, unemployment had doubled, and stood at 23 per cent. The desperateness of the unemployed led to hustling of one kind or another — petty trading in food and ganja, gambling, prostitution and eventually robbery and other kinds of crime.

1. Capitalist Development and JLP Repression

While the economy continued to grow at high rates — though slower than during the 1950's — the maldistribution of wealth and income rapidly became more intolerable. The benefits of economic growth made fortunes for foreign and local capitalists; and swelled the numbers as well as the incomes of the professional and salaried sections of the middle class and a small upper stratum of the working class. Here and there, in the cracks of this increasingly monopolistic economy, small businesses established by enterprising Jamaicans survived with varying degrees of success. On the other hand, the social misery and frustration of the masses grew apace with the accumulation of wealth by the bourgeoisie. The contrast between wealth and poverty was visibly displayed in the Kingston Metropolitan Area as mansions climbed up the hillsides while ghettoes spawned along Spanish Town Road. Furthermore, improved medical standards — private and public — together with the closing of emigration outlets led to important demographic shifts in the age structure of the population, with the youth — under 29 years accounting for a larger and larger share.

Externally, the economy became even more firmly wedded to the imperialist system, as foreign ownership and control grew. In anticipation and in reaction to national sentiments against foreign ownership, foreign capitalists sought new ways of exercising indirect control, such as joint partnerships and technology and management contracts with Jamaican capitalists. In addition, there was continuous Jamaicanization of technical and management personnel of foreign companies, although this was generally restricted to elite ethnic groups.

These economic developments formed the basis for the policies of the JLP regime. Externally, Jamaica lined up behind the big capitalist countries on most international issues. Perhaps the only exceptions were issues relating to South African apartheid and to the economic and political isolation of Cuba.

Domestic policy was increasingly repressive. Progressive and radical political activists were harassed (passports seized), intimidated, jailed and deported. Progressive and socialist literature, culture and activities were banned. Rastafari bore the brunt of cultural repression from a regime whose consciousness must have been tormented by the challenge Rastafari represented to the oppressive social order. Thus the economic oppression of the masses was supported by the political and cultural repression of the State. The Youth, in particular, were brutalized by a regime and a social system which was incapable of channeling their creative energies into productive activities, and instead regarded them as superfluous and a social and political nuisance.

Whereas the JLP had come to power in 1962 with the support of a broad alliance of classes, the policies it pursued as well as spontaneous changes in the world economy over which it had no control, ultimately eroded the basis of its support. In fact the alliance was probably eroded by 1967, for the JLP returned to power on the basis of massive electoral fraud and disenfranchisement of young voters.

Rising social discontent took many forms. There was of course, the spontaneous breakdown of social life, as anti-social behaviour — crime, hustling, corruption in government — grew. But more important were the political challenges to the hegemony of the JLP and the class interests it now served from three main sources. There was the growth of radical nationalist and socialist political groups particularly among the middle-class intelligentsia. There was Rastafari, resisting the cultural oppression of the African that sanctioned the economic exploitation of the black workers and peasants. Finally, there was the reorganization of the PNP under Michael Manley.

All of this, of course, occurs in the context of dramatic and historic changes in the balance of political forces internationally. In the decade of the '60's imperialism — the U.S.A., in particular, suffered major political defeats around the world, especially in Cuba (Bay of Pigs) and in Indo-China.

In contrast, the rise of the prestige of the national liberation movements and the world socialist movement exposed regimes like the JLP in Jamaica, to ridicule in the eyes of its own people.

2. Resistance to JLP Repression

The political response to the JLP repression took many forms. There were various nationalist groups and organizations, many of which came together behind the Abeng Newspaper. Many of these groups were formed by radical intellectuals of middle-class backgrounds. Through them, the militance of the Black Power Movement in the U.S.A. and the revolutionary slogans of the National Liberation Movements of the world, fed into the mass struggle.

More important, some revolutionary intellectuals began to study Marxism and socialist revolutions, despite a ban on such literature by the JLP government. For them the Cuban revolution posed a real alternative to the capitalist dependent under-development of the Puerto Rican model.

Yet another response was the dramatic growth of Rastafari, and the culture of Dread spawned by it. Recall that Rastafari had emerged as a social movement immediately after the Coronation of Selassie as Emperor. For them he was the second coming of the Messiah, Jah, and at one and the same time the rejection and reaffirmation of Christianity. Jah in his blackness negated the whiteness of Jesus; in his living he negated the death of Jesus by Crucifixion. He was the symbol of resistance to the white christian church, in which the power to oppress black people, was thought to reside. Rastafari went behind Christianity as it were into the Old Testament and identified the Black Jamaicans as the chosen people of which the Bible spoke. In the bondage and oppression of the Hebrews in Egypt, they saw their own bondage and oppression in this latter day Babylon. And just as the Bible spoke of the return of the people of Israel from exile to their homeland, so too the Rastafari saw repatriation to Ethiopia/Africa as the escape from Babylon.

In their rejection of Christianity as the philosophy of the (white) oppressors, Rastafari drew heavily on the teachings of Marcus Garvey, whom they hailed as prophet. It was Garvey who posed the problem of national oppression of the

African peoples of the Americas, and Jamaica in particular, most sharply and concretely. His solution was repatriation to Africa and Rastafari embraced it.

Nevertheless, Rastafari reaffirmed the basic principles and teachings of Christianity through the substitution of an African for a European Messiah. As before, liberation from oppression was delegated to the Messiah. This reaffirmation/rejection of Christianity synthesis with Garveyism manifested itself in the ambiguities of Rastafarian reasoning, discourse and social analysis. Eventually, in the '70's, there began to emerge sects which adopted fundamentalist interpretations of the Bible while neglecting the political content of Garveyism.

In the last chapter, we showed how the PNP jettisoned its progressive character by purging its Marxist wing. It was not until the end of the post-independence decade that the PNP under Manley-the-younger began to champion the cause of the toiling and oppressed masses. The vacuum had been filled by Rastafari, its very social existence being a negation of the ways of the dominant society of Babylon. In rejecting society, Rastafari also rejected wage labour in favour of independent occupations like fishing, handicrafts, ganja trading, and general hustling. Probably this tendency derived from the fact that up to this time the Rastafari tended to be displaced peasants, or people otherwise socially disoriented in urban society on account of their rural ties.

The influence of Rastafari nevertheless went beyond their numbers and beyond the social origins from which they came. It especially permeated the unemployed as well as some of the middle class youth. It was obviously an attractive ideology to the unemployed so far as it denounced the society that marginalized them. Its militant and strident language was used to denounce Babylon in song. It was attractive to the alienated children of the middle class. Many of them were sensitive to their ambiguous place in a sharply divided society; not rich, but not poor, in fact not far better off than the masses; neither black, nor white, but rejecting the dominant white culture which served to alienate them from the black masses. The reaffirmation of their Africanness and the reinterpretation of their Christianity as a philosophy of social protest made Rastafari a ready ideology for coping with their socio-cultural alienation.

Eventually, Rastafari spawned a broader counter-culture, the culture of Dread, embracing various nationalist tendencies. Its symbols and cultural values were adopted by many who never quite accepted, or even rejected, its theological content, its worship of Selassie and its commitment to repatriation. They became symbols of protest against the political, economic and cultural oppression of foreign capital and its local allies in the Jamaican bourgeoisie. So much so, that in reasserting leadership of the people's struggles, Manley and the PNP utilized many of the symbols of Rastafari, even to the point of identifying Manley with the Biblical Joshua.

Finally, there was the reorganization of the PNP under Manley-the-younger. The PNP has always regarded itself as the leader of the National Movement. By that it means that it has been the vanguard in articulating the aspirations of the Jamaican people for nationhood and independence. Of course, the PNP never had sufficient ideological clarity to specify which sections of the population, which classes, would benefit from the kind of independence the party sought. Certainly, this claim lost its validity in the aftermath of the purge of its communist cadres in 1952 and revealed the true class basis of the PNP — i.e. a party dominated by the mulatto petit-bourgeoisie. Thereafter, as we have pointed out in an earlier chapter, the PNP drew closer ideologically to the JLP, as the right wing of the petty bourgeoisie — Glasspole, Isaacs, etc. — gained ascendancy in the party.

The bankruptcy of the political system and particularly the politics of the PNP became evident in the 1960's. It was also evident that unless the PNP could channel all the progressive and radical political tendencies in the society into a coherent movement, it could never win mass support to unseat the JLP. Accordingly, Michael Manley carefully constructed a broad alliance of the nationalist and progressive elements within the local bourgeoisie, progressive elements of the middle class whose liberal political sentiments had been outraged by JLP repression, workers, peasants, unemployeds and other disaffected strata, such as youth and Rastafari.

The PNP victory of 1972, therefore, was a coming together of three important currents: the radicalism of the youth and particularly the progressive intelligentsia, the cultural mass movement emanating out of the Rastafari, and the reorganization of the PNP as a mass political party. Once again the PNP claimed leadership of the National Movement, now with widespread popular support. The use and abuse of this mandate goes a far way in explaining the rise and demise of the PNP in the 1970's.

3. The Social Economy

The Jamaican economy can be best described as a dependent capitalist economy. It functions as a peripheral attachment to the international capitalist system. That system consists of central (metropolitan) economies, like the United States of America, which extract surpluses from the peripheral (Third World) economies like Jamaica. Surplus extraction derives from ownership of Third World resources, from the "unequal exchange" in trade, from interest charged on loans, from management services provided, and from royalties and fees charged for technology. Together, these constitute a substantial drain on the productive potential of Third World countries. The Multinational Corporations (MNC), international lending agencies like the IMF and World Bank (IBRD) and metropolitan governments are the institutional mechanisms which effect transfers of the surplus. To the extent that some of the surplus is reinvested in the country, this increases the economic power of foreign capital and this enhances its political power in the "body politics" of the dependent country. Thus capitalism on a world scale simultaneously generates economic growth (development) of central metropolitan economies and economic retardation (underdevelopment) of the peripheral economies. The two results are linked. They stem from the nature of capitalism as a world system.

The Jamaican economy depends on the central economies of the United States of America, Western Europe (chiefly the United Kingdom), Canada and Japan for trade, finance, technology and management. Most of Jamaica's wealth is owned by capitalists in the United States of America, Canada and the United Kingdom. As a result, the Jamaican economy is disjointed. The national economy is weak and underdeveloped because land and capital are concentrated in the export economy which is, moreover, predominantly under foreign control. Labour is concentrated in the national economy where land and capital are in limited supply. In these circumstances, under-employment is endemic. And foreign capital benefits from massive surpluses as a result of the fact that the reserve army of labour allows capitalists to keep wages relatively low.

Jamaican society exhibits a mass of contradictions which are institutionalized in the structure of the economy. On close examination, we find that the Jamaican economy consists of a functionally disconnected national economy which has grown up as an appendage of, and in the interstices of, a foreign-oriented and dominated export economy. And the common theme that runs through the two aspects of the Jamaican economy is the exploitation of labour by property.

The contradictions which constitute Jamaican economy and society are obvious. We produce for the consumption of white people in Europe and North America and consume the fruits of their labour. The prices of their goods go up, while ours go down. Those who earn the foreign exchange for Jamaica (workers and peasants) consume a relatively small part of it. Those who produce material wealth for the society earn much less income than those who perform ancillary services, some of which are necessary, like the distribution of goods; some of which are not, like insurance. Given the high rate of inflation and the low rate of interest, the real savings of peasants and workers over time are negative; so that the net effect is a subsidy to the profits of the capitalist class. In general, our resources are not fully utilised for the benefit of the people. Instead, they are largely exploited by foreign capitalists and the small client (comprador) class of Jamaican capitalists. The fundamental contradiction, of which these and others are but manifestations, is the contradiction between property and labour. It is this central contradiction which ultimately explains why our resources are used the way they are; and also determines what, and how, different groups of people in our society benefit from the changes over time.

The contradiction between property (first as merchant, capital and land; later as finance and manufacturing capital) and labour, was discussed earlier. In fact, *it is the development of this central contradiction which constitutes the core of our historical experience.* Structurally and institutionally, this contradiction manifests itself in the following ways.

First, our exporting industries are thoroughly tied to the advanced capitalist countries. They are tied through the use of imported employment, technology, raw materials, foreign finance and foreign markets. This is the case, to one degree or another, for bauxite and alumina, sugar, tourism and manufacturing. And the majority share of the financial system — commercial banks, insurance companies, etc. — is foreign-owned. It operates to facilitate a certain skewed pattern of production. It means that our people and our resources are exploited through high prices for what we buy and low prices for what we sell.

But while thoroughly integrated with the advanced capitalist economies, these industries are largely disconnected from the national economy. Thus we neither process alumina nor sugar. We do not, for the most part, use the hotels nor do the hotels utilise any significant share of the commodities we produce. The predominant activity that passes for manufacturing is merely the assembly of imported parts, and therefore, it utilises little local labour.

Second, the national economy depends almost entirely on the level of activity in the export industries. When Revere goes, the businesses and farms in Maggotty and the surrounding countryside are forced to contract or close. Similarly, when the tourists do not come, Montego Bay is by definition in a state of crisis because it is a "pure tourist" economy.

However, not all of the national economy is directly dependent. There are numerous small businesses, a few large manufacturers and hundreds of thousands of small peasants who utilise local raw materials in the production of goods for local consumption. Add to that, the myriad of petty trading and hustling activities (legal and illegal) without which the masses of our unemployed could not survive. The growth of production in the national economy has been stifled largely through the ownership of our resources by the foreign capitalists. Land and finance are not available to the small peasant farmer who, therefore, cannot produce sufficient food to feed the nation. And why? Because land and finance are monopolised by the agrarian capitalists, the foreign monopolies, such as the bauxite companies and the banks. Furthermore, the tools and fertilisers needed by the farmer, if he could get the land and finance, are imported at high prices.

Similarly, our small businessmen are unable to raise finance, since the banking system does not cater to the small man. Worse, they are forced to buy raw materials at exorbitant retail prices from the merchant, who then markets the finished products at a substantial profit for himself. And so, only a marginal return accrues to the small businessman. Actually, the small businessman finances the large merchant in so far as he receives payment for his product after it has been sold. Many a recent bankruptcy has resulted from the unpatriotic merchants who have fled the country with the money of small manufacturer/craftsmen (e.g. furniture makers). Add to that the fact that the small businessman faces severe competition from imports and/or from large firms utilising foreign finance and technology. The desire of the small businessman for economic independence remains an illusion; for in effect, only his labour stands between the raw material supplied by the merchant and the product marketed, sometimes by the same merchant.

The system is such that partly because resources are immobilised by foreign and local capitalists, partly because capital-intensive techniques are favoured by businessmen who wish to minimise the use of "uncontrollable" labour, and partly because the capitalists are unwilling to invest much of their profits in Jamaica (even under guarantee from the State), many of our people are unemployed. So that we have the seemingly curious situation of idle lands, idle machinery and idle labour existing side by side; while our people are desperately short of food and other vital necessities. The creativity of our people, born out of struggle for survival, has allowed them to exist on the margins of the productive economy, by selling their services, engaging in petty trading of consumer goods, and hustling of all sorts. These activities sometimes cut across the frontiers of legality; but, even so, they must be squarely faced as genuine economic activities.

We have been reasoning around two themes — firstly, the integration of the export and import (branch-plant manufacturing) industries into advanced capitalist economies through the agency of foreign capital. The second is the dependent but disarticulated and disjointed character of the national economy. We now consider how these themes are reflected at another level of the social system. Specifically, we examine some aspects of the role of the State in the economy.

4. The State and Class Interests

The modern Jamaican state is in a process of transition from a role designed exclusively to service the interests of foreign capitalists and the national white (and near-white) capitalist class. The struggle for national independence has meant a gradual shift in political power towards more democratic control by the black masses of peasants and the working class and by patriotic elements in the bourgeoisie and the petit-bourgeoisie. Needless to say, this tendency must not be exaggerated. But more and more the state is brought to service the needs of such an alliance of social classes and less and less the interests of foreign capital. So foreign capital is forced to form a tactical alliance with the national (private and state) capitalist class to produce a client (comprador) class, or better yet, a *"lumpen bourgeoisie"*.

Nevertheless, the present Jamaican state is decisively in the service of the propertied rather than the property-less. There has been a strategy of subsidising and protecting big capital — foreign and local — through legislation which has not yet run its course. As testimony, we cite the Incentive Legislation for the repatriation of profits to the head offices (bauxite companies and banks), and current legislation circumscribing the right of workers to strike. The state has provided finance, building and institutions to service big capital, through the auspices of the JIDC and related institutions. This meant that, for the most part, aspects of the state dealing with the exporting industries are highly developed.

On the other hand, since the thrust of government policy has hardly been toward small businessmen and small farmers, workers and unemployed, those aspects dealing with the national economy are highly underdeveloped. Legislation protecting the small businessman and the small farmer from exploitative prices, unfair trading practices, onerous loan terms, and competition with big capital is yet to be written. Specialised state institutions, such as SEDCO, and ADC are virtually ineffective; and, in some cases, these institutions are actually obstacles to the development of the national economy. Others, such as JDB and WSLB, have tended to allocate their resources according to the objective laws of the system; and, therefore, much of their resources do not flow to the small businesses and farms. State support for sectors of the economy mirrors the pattern of the national economy: disarticulated, disjointed and underdeveloped. How far the state is oriented toward the development of the national economy depends directly on the struggle for national independence and a simultaneous disengagement from imperialism.

These two themes — integration with the advanced central capitalist economies through the agency of foreign capital, and the disarticulated disjointedness of the national economy — are reflected in all spheres of our social life; whether it be the education system, the health system or the cultural patterns of our people. They in turn are explained by the central contradiction between capital and labour. More specifically, the character of the economy is determined by the exploitation of the labour of our people and the resources of our country and the subservience of the national capitalist class to foreign capital.

5. Political Parties and Class Interests

When we speak of the *class character* of a political party, we refer to the class composition of its membership, particularly the leadership, and the class interests it pursues through its policies, and programmes. In this sense, the class character of a party will change over time, reflecting realignments and the growth of the various classes in society.

Both PNP and the JLP have shared this basic class characteristic: they have predominantly been petit-bourgeois parties. The JLP had for many years, until 1974, the mass of peasant support, hardly on account of its programmes, but more on account of Bustamante's charisma and "roots-ness". This, in turn, was reinforced by the alienation of the masses from the quasi-aristocratic and socially aloof leadership of the PNP under Manley-the-elder. The PNP, on the other hand, commanded the support of the mulatto petit-bourgeoisie, the middle class professionals and functionaries. So much so in fact, that they could be successfully stigmatized by the JLP as a "brown-man" party. Thus if the **petit-**

bourgeoisie is composed of big and middle peasants, own-account independent producers and small businessmen, and the brown middle class, then the JLP commanded the support of the majority of the former two strata, while the PNP commanded the support of the last. Both parties' leadership cadres were drawn primarily from the brown petit-bourgeoisie.

Both parties have been based on unions from their inception. The JLP's BITU is older and larger than the PNP's NWU and TUC, though the latter made tremendous gains during the JLP era 1962-1972. Whereas the BITU has had a strong agro-proletariat and casual service worker base, the NWU/TUC draws its strength from workers in manufacturing and mining. The most recent wave of unionization has been among the upper strata of the working class such as bank clerks, office clerks, civil servants, etc., and even among the managerial strata. Not surprisingly, it is the BITU which had made most gains in this phase, coming as it did during the recent PNP era of 1972-1979.

These unions have tended to be economistic and opportunistic. In fact, aided and abetted by the anti-communist propaganda and support of the North American union movement, they have tended to oppose progressive and socialist programmes except where they fit into narrow economistic interests. This failure to represent the real interests of workers facilitated a proliferation of independent unions in the 1960's and 1970's, which have been unable to break the hegemony of the BITU-NWU-TUC over the organized labour movement.

The ruling class has divided its support between the two parties. Except for a brief historical moment, 1972-1974, when the PNP picked up the support of the newest strata of the capitalist class, it has been the JLP which enjoyed the greater share of capitalist support. Certainly the old oligarchy of big planters and merchants have remained solidly behind the JLP. Developments of the late 1950's and 1960's created a new strata of modern-day client capitalists, many of whom displayed a tenacious patriotism. It is the fickle support of this strata of the capitalist class that the PNP won in 1972 and lost by 1979.

Finally, the developments of the 60's created a mass of unemployed, a small but disruptive lumpen proletariat and many displaced rural migrants forced to engage in a hustle existence within the cities and towns, particularly in Kingston. Additionally, demographic shifts produced a growing youth population which could not be productively accommodated within the social economy. Frustrated by the lack of opportunities and alienated by the political and cultural oppression of the JLP regime, this strata supported the PNP's "Better-must-come"/"Power for the People" campaign and contributed to its decisive victories at the polls in 1972 and again in 1976.

CHAPTER 8

DEMOCRATIC SOCIALISM, STRUGGLE AND CHANGE 1974 – 1979

The 1972 election campaign of the PNP was mounted on two slogans: "Better Must Come" and "Power for the People". (We think that "for" is significant since it reflects that party's elitist conception of fitness to rule deriving from colonial days. What is required is power *to* the people). The party had galvanized an alliance of the dispossessed but did not provide a positive plan for change. It capitalized on the corruption of the former JLP regime and the degree to which race and class divisions within the JLP had undermined the authority of the government. The Shearer regime was split from within. Seaga and Lightbourne, representing the white bourgeoisie, were intolerable of a black working-class type prime minister and administered their ministerial portfolios more or less independently. While Wilton Hill, representing the brown/black petit-bourgeoisie, set up his own housing empire (a "corporation-sole"). Shearer, the country's only ever black prime minister, with his trade union background, was literally hounded out of office.

The new Manley PNP regime of 1972 introduced a number of significant social reforms while maintaining the traditional PNP-JLP economic policy of industrialization by invitation. The social reforms ("people programmes") galvanized the alliance of dispossessed and heightened perspectives to a stage that forced the party to articulate a "democratic socialist" ideology in late 1974. External events relating to successful liberation struggles elsewhere provided further stimulus.

Henceforth, and for the first time in Jamaican party politics, an ideological distinction could be made between the two contending parties. The period 1974-76 marks a watershed in the history of Jamaican politics. For socialism became legitimised in the political process for the first time; and this put the class question on the agenda of what up to then, was nothing more than the politics of tweedle-dum and tweedle-dee.

1. Economic Crisis and the Response

The present crisis in the international capitalist system is characterised by rising prices along with rising unemployment in the industrial centre countries. Capitalist economy always moves through short periods of boom and recession (the so-called business cycle) and through longer periods of expansion and structural crisis. While the 1950's and 1960's witnessed historically unprecedented economic growth of the industrialized capitalist countries, and indeed of the international capitalist system, the momentum of growth slowed down throughout the 1970's and is expected to remain slow in the 1980's.

The current crisis of international capitalism began at the end of the 1960's and deepened during the 1970's as a result of the following:

(i) The victory of the Vietnamese people over U.S. imperialism put a brakes on the expansion of the U.S. economy which was being fueled by war production for decades (World War II, Cold War, Korean War, then Vietnam). Additionally this defeat contributed to a chronic drain of gold out of the U.S.; and, in 1971, forced that 'top metropole' to suspend the convertibility of its currency to gold. And so came the end of a stable international monetary system.

(ii) Japan and Western Europe (especially West Germany) having fully recovered from the effects of World War II began to challenge the hegemony of the U.S.A. for markets and resources within the international capitalist system. The resulting dramatic exchange rate adjustments between the U.S. dollar, the mark and the yen further reduced the viability of the U.S. dollar as *the* international reserve currency.

(iii) Within the industrialized capitalist countries, domestic credit expansion as a means of combatting the 'natural' recessions of capitalism set off a series of wage-price spirals that accentuated the rate of inflation.

(iv) Faced with rising import prices, raw material exporting Third World nations began to assert their authority in the market by forming cartels. The most significant of these was OPEC which started to increase oil prices in 1973. And because of the importance of oil this action further aggravated inflationary trends and international monetary instability.

(v) Acceleration of the process of decolonization with the rapid succession of victorious socialist revolutions in Africa and Asia throughout the 1970's brought about a dramatic shift in the balance of forces in the world. This weakened the hegemonic control of imperialism over Third World resources and markets and, simultaneously, heightened the struggle for altering the domination-dependence relations between the centre and periphery of the international capitalist system.

Third World countries have suffered severe dislocations as a result of this crisis of capitalism. Most of them were unable to cushion their economies in the manner of the oil-exporting countries. Other raw material cartels like the IBA for bauxite and UBEC for bananas could not match the achievements of OPEC. Faced with consistent import price increases (including oil) and declining export earnings Third World countries accumulated huge trade deficits. And, in varying degrees, they fell into balance of payments difficulties. This forced them to borrow from the international banks and the IMF. The resulting astronomical rise in the indebtedness of Third World nations is an important factor in stepping up the struggle for a "new international economic order".

It is against this background that we must view Jamaica's experience during the 1970's. The structure of the Jamaican economy makes it extremely vulnerable to external developments. Accordingly the current crisis hit us for six. Falling export earnings coupled with rising import prices put a tight squeeze on our capacity to import. Rising import prices pushed up our cost of living dramatically, thus lowering the real incomes of the masses of poor people. Foreign capital inflows declined during the recession of 1974-75 and so fewer job opportunities were created. Government expenditure had to expand to accommodate legitimate demands for wage increases in the public sector while private sector wages also increased. This created a fiscal crisis (i.e. excess of government expenditure over government revenues) and a balance of payments crisis (i.e. excess of foreign payments over foreign receipts).

1974–1976

The struggle against imperialism came to a head when the Manley regime initiated an assault to rescue Jamaica from the crisis. The following measures stand out:

    (a) the Bauxite Levy to increase government revenue and the country's foreign exchange receipts from the bauxite/alumina industry;

    (b) formation of the International Bauxite Association (IBA) in which Manley was instrumental;

    (c) numerous social welfare measures and programmes like SEP for poor people employment, PLL for peasant farmers, the minimum wage for workers; and

    (d) raising the level of socialist political consciousness in order to support the assault.

    (e) On the level of international relations, the regime strengthened and firmed up relations with neighbouring socialist Cuba;

    (f) provided *active* support for the liberation struggles in Southern Africa (the backing of Cuban armed assistance in the Angola resistance was particularly aggravating to U.S. imperialists); and

    (g) helped to fortify the Non-Aligned Movement and the struggle for a New International Economic Order (NIEO).

The reaction of imperialism and the national capitalist class to these initiatives was, and continues to be, hostile. Coming at a time when the top metropole suffered its first final military defeat at the hands of the Vietnamese people in 1975 along with the rest of Indo-China, i.e. Laos and Cambodia (Kampuchea); at a time when Angola, Mozambique, and Guinea-Bissau won revolutionary independence from Portugal in 1976; and with Ethiopia bubbling with socialist revolution in the Horn of Africa 1974-75, imperialism viewed the threatening clouds of similar situations in the Caribbean with expected alarm.

Retaliation was predictable. These came in the overt form of:

(a) reduction in bauxite production;

(b) credit blockade by the U.S.A. in March 1976;

(c) foreign press attacks to destroy tourism, throughout 1976;

(d) flight of capital, and the migration of sections of the bourgeois, petit-bourgeois and professional classes;

(e) go-slow in production and the refusal to undertake new investments by a wide strata of the capitalist class which remained in Jamaica;

and, finally, in the covert acts of

(f) destabilization engineered by the U.S. Central Intelligence Agency (CIA).

In terms of party politics imperialism found a ready ally in the Seaga-led JLP. Seaga's accession to leadership of that party after the demise of Shearer, placed a firmer stamp of reaction on the traditional JLP of leaders like Bustamante/Shearer/Newland coming out of a trade union base. Representing more openly the interest of the white and near-white capitalist class, Seaga presented a trusted ally to imperialism and he built up a capacity for national mobilization on an alleged competence in state financial management.

2. Resistance and Petit-bourgeois Capitulation

The retaliation of imperialism in the period 1974-76 to the initiatives taken by government on behalf of poor people incensed the masses. And the PNP launched a national anti-imperialist campaign that fired the spirit of resistance throughout 1976. Other progressive groups like the WLL weighed in, and a genuine *national* movement consolidated itself. So much so that the opposition JLP was forced to adopt "nationalism" as its contending ideology.

Michael Manley reflected the mood of the Jamaican people in his National Stadium speech of September 1976 when he articulated the view that WE ARE NOT FOR SALE,

WE KNOW WHERE WE ARE GOING! C.L.R. James wrote of that speech as follows:

> "I would like to say that in fifty years of political activity and interest in all sorts of politics, I have never heard or read a speech more defiant of oppression and in every political way more suitable to its purpose."

That is the testimony of a man who has been a central figure in Pan-Africanism and the decolonization of the Black World since the 1930's. It cannot be taken lightly!

What happened in the six months that followed that speech is of central importance. For by March of 1977 Manley had turned in the opposite direction and sold Jamaica to imperialism and its central bank, the IMF. That act initiated a process that generated the most severe economic sufferation Jamaicans have experienced in living memory. After three long years of that adversity the rank and file of the PNP finally forced the government to expel the IMF in March 1980. This was indeed a watershed in the history of Jamaican politics. For it is the first time that an official decision came to be made by the popular dictate of the masses.

The national mood, tempo and tone of resistance mounted after that September 1976 speech with a strong anti-imperialist electoral campaign waged by the PNP with the support of the WLL, CPJ and other progressive groups. On December 15, 1976 the electorate gave the PNP a resounding mandate to move the country forward on a path toward self-reliant *democratic socialism.* In two speeches made to the nation in January 1977, Prime Minister Manley clearly articulated his government's positive response to that mandate. He commissioned the National Planning Agency to prepare an Emergency Production Plan for 1977 in the spirit of the electoral mandate.

The Planning Agency in turn invited the public to send in ideas. And the response was tremendous. Tens of thousands of ideas and suggestions from the public poured into the government planning and mobilization agencies. All the proposals indicated concrete ways in which greater reliance on our own resources could be achieved. The de-stabilization measures of imperialism seemed to galvanize the people's resolve to struggle harder.

In an appendix, we outline the zigs and zags of government policy in 1977 in response to the contending political forces within the PNP and the implicit national alliance it led. This period is deserving of deeper analysis since it exhibits so clearly the contradictions of race and class which permeate the society as a whole and the PNP in particular, and which are personified in Michael Manley. By mid-1977, the government capitulated to imperialism by signing an agreement with the IMF for balance of payment support. And after that, popular support for the Manley regime withered dramatically. The IMF seal of approval for external support generated such a massive decline of the standard of living of the working class that internal support weakened consistently.

The period January to March of 1977 was critical. The question remains unanswered as to what factors triggered the turn-back of Prime Minister Manley from his January commitment to a self-reliant democratic socialist path? We are of the view that the fundamental explanation lies in his lack of confidence in the capacity of the masses of black Jamaican people to assert their productive creativity. It is a position that derives from a brown Jamaican petit-bourgeois perspective. As we indicated in Chapter 1, individuals are a product of their own history, and man's social consciousness is determined by his social being.

There were, of course, other factors at work as well. The class character of the government (especially the Cabinet) constrained the possibilities of trying to break with international capitalism. Hence early attempts made in January to seek external assistance from the socialist bloc of countries in Europe were sabotaged and frustrated by March. Meanwhile, several treks were made to Washington seeking assistance from the new Carter administration.

In his April 22, 1977 presentation to parliament, Manley abandoned the *Peoples' Plan* formulated by the public and the Planning Agency and announced that government would begin negotiations with the IMF for balance of payments support. The stage was set to take the country deeper into the net of international capitalism.

3. The Politics of Change — 1977-79

During the three years of IMF governance, zig-zag politics of the Manley regime hindered the peoples' struggle for progress and strengthened the hand of imperialism in alliance with the local capitalist class and the Seaga-led JLP.

Soon after Manley's national broadcasts of January 1977 rallying the nation to a self-reliant socialist path, the new regime started to deviate back to a capitalist path. A new administration had been installed in the U.S.A. with Carter at the head and with alleged Jamaican "friends" like Andrew Young as part of his team. After a limited and tentative attempt to secure economic assistance from the socialist countries in January 1977, the regime shifted its focus to seeking help from the new U.S.A. administration. Already the local capitalist class responded to the early January 1977 socialist stance by a slow-down of business activities and the banking system introduced selective credit. The flight of capital in the 1976 mobilization had left the central bank with virtually no foreign exchange by December 1976. And the government was forced to close off trading in foreign exchange until the situation was brought under control.

In April 1977, government capitulated, and sought assistance from the IMF which dragged out the negotiations until July when an agreement was signed, allowing for devaluation of 40% with a two-tier exchange rate that maintained the old rate for certain basic goods. That agreement was short lived. In December 1977, the IMF suspended the agreement on a technicality. The Fund then prolonged negotiations for a new agreement from January to May 1978 so as to bring the country to the brink of defaulting on foreign debts. Government, in this weak bargaining position and with a dissipated mass internal support, had no choice but to accept the extremely harsh terms of a new agreement. This three-year agreement involved another massive devaluation (15% immediately with unification of the exchange rate and monthly devaluations to total a further 15% in the first year; wage restraint with a ceiling of 15%; guaranteed profits for the private sector with a floor of 20%; a cutback in operations of the State Trading Corporation; and tight budget management to restrict government expenditures and participation in the economy along with a projected $180 million new taxes).

The consequent 40% increase in the cost of living and the 15% ceiling on wages meant a 25% cut in the real wages of the employed working class *in a single year*. This set the stage for such a scale of disaffection that by January 1979, the opposition JLP was able to mobilize mass protests. A gas price increase was used as a pretext for a road-block demonstration which received such popular support across party lines that both political parties hurriedly put a stop to it. The road-block protest of January 8-10, 1979 demonstrated in the clearest terms that the social base of the December 1976 PNP electoral victory had been eroded.

The castration of the left-wing of the party in September 1977 was part of the price Manley was forced to pay to secure IMF support. And with the January 1979 demonstration of the erosion of the base of the 1976 victory, Manley was forced to put in place a plan to rehabilitate his left-wing which alone has the capacity for mass mobilization. Meanwhile the opposition JLP proceeded to organize a "day of peace and protest" in March with a call for a one-day strike by employers who should pay workers to stay at home. The response to that effort was only partly successful because organized labour, including the BITU, did not support it.

Progressive forces outside of the PNP led the struggle against imperialism during these three-years of IMF rule. The Marxist Workers Liberation League (WLL) became a political party in December 1978 and as the Workers Party of Jamaica (WPJ) entered the electoral arena. It began attracting a substantial section of disaffected youth and intensified its political education campaign. By the end of 1979 the WPJ had a significant 4-5% standing in electoral polls. The WLL-WPJ was the main organizational force in the three-year struggle against imperialism when the zig-zag politics of Manley put the PNP. left in disarray and put the credibility of Manley as leader of the national left forces squarely on the line. The other organizations within the socialist movement, like the Communist Party of Jamaica (CPJ), Youth Forces for National Liberation (YFNL), are relatively small and less articulate in public discourse.

Severe ideological differences originating in the Sino-Soviet struggle were imported into the people's struggles by uncritical ideological alignment to one or the other antagonistic poles in the world socialist movement. Needless to say, this served to undermine any coherent anti-imperialist alliance which became more and more necessary as the PNP forfeited its leadership role.

On the whole, the "socialist" forces within the body politics are divided by sectarianism, personality conflicts, and opportunism. Consequently, there is little or no effort at consolidation. Diagram 8.1 provides a synoptic view of the balance of political forces in 1979. It demonstrates that the 'progressive left' is fragmented and depends exclusively on whatever leadership Michael Manley provides them. It is extremely important to note that:

(i) only a small number of the PNP parliamentary group are on the side of the progressive left (only 3-7 of the 47);

(ii) there is a sharp cleavage between the PNP left and the communists (the extra-party left);

(iii) sectarianism prevails among the communists;

(iv) there is an excessive dependence of the communists, particularly the WPJ, on the leadership of Manley in what they describe as "critical support".

Accordingly, Manley assumes undisputed importance as leader of the 'progressive movement' while presiding over a government and party that is overwhelmingly reactionary.

This contradiction contributes to consistent disarticulation of the progressive left. In marked contrast the forces of reaction are consolidated and strong. The majority of the PNP parliamentary group and that party's affiliated trade unions have only a tribal disconnection from the reactionary opposition JLP and its affiliated union. In these circumstances, there are institutional blockages that inhibit the articulation of the aspirations of the masses of workers and peasants for liberation from the oppressive conditions generated by capitalism and imperialism.

4. Black Affirmation and Struggle

The IMF solution (?) locked the Jamaican economy tighter in the prison of the international capitalist system and this increased the pressure on the working class and the peasantry. The unionized section of the working class strug-

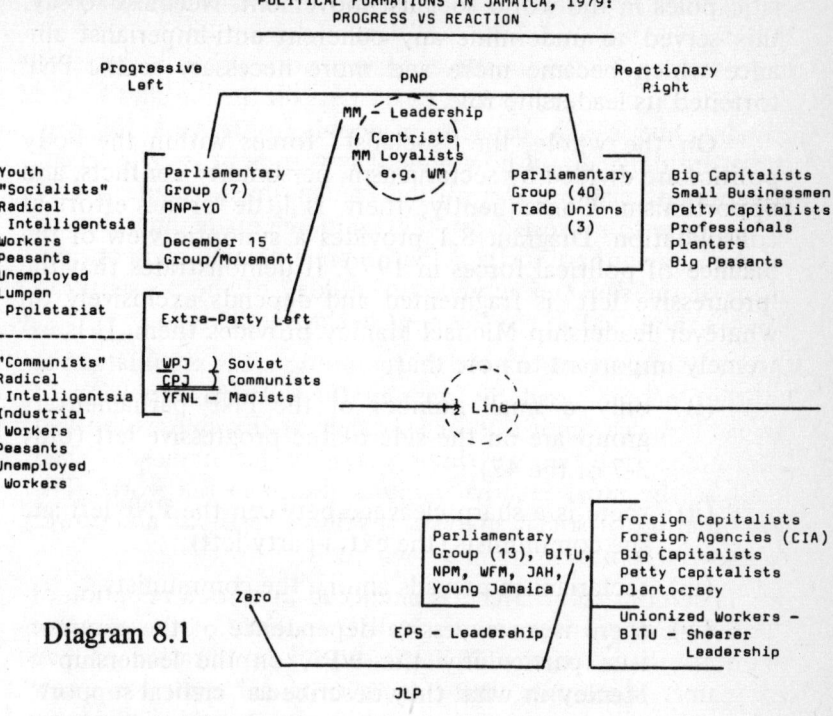

Diagram 8.1

gled against the tide. And in spite of shortages of critical imported inputs (e.g. machettes, files, fertilizers) peasant output of food expanded dramatically. Between December 1976 and December 1978, for example, while the total output of the economy fell 6% the output of "domestic agriculture" increased some 10-20%. The lower strata of the non-unionized working class ('displaced peasantry') struggled against the worsening economic conditions by increasing various types of hustle activities.

Shortages of imported consumer items created openings for unprecedented growth of the hustle economy. For example some higglers began to purchase foodstuffs like skellion and ground provisions from peasant farmers for sale overseas in places like Cayman and Panama. Out of the proceeds, they then purchase items like cornflakes and clothing, bring these back to Jamaica and retail at prices which realise them substantial profit. So as big merchant stores like Hanna's folded in the crisis, sidewalk vendors prospered right in front of their doors. The merchant class are no longer Kings on King Street.

In times of capitalist crisis, the hustle economy assumes major importance in the political economy of survival. A large segment of the hustle economy normally is illegal, like ganja production and trade; or borders on the illegal, like the 'Panama hustle'. The capacity of people to survive in this way therefore depends on how lenient government is. The recent government clamp down on the Panama hustle came largely in response to protests from the big merchant/manufacturers. Modern day urban hustle activities are a parallel and continuation of the squatter survival technology of the peasantry in Bogle's time, and of the Maroons in slavery days.

The deepening capitalist economic crisis stimulates yet another people-based response in the cultural explosion of 'Dread'. Reggae music is one branch of this expression and during the last two or three years, reggae has established itself as the most creative popular music in the world. The combination of social analysis, rhythmic aesthetic and power of expression has no equal anywhere.

The culture of Dread is anchored in a total rejection of "Babylonian" (western capitalist) society, of its value orientations and mode of life based on exploitation of man by man. Accordingly, the culture of dread embraces a new morality and a new philosophy of brotherhood, of harmony with Nature in the production process, and of communal modes of existence. And the assertion of Africanity generates a pride of ancestry and African cultural traditions. The culture of Dread, therefore, represents a powerful base for the economic and political liberation of the black masses of workers and peasants.

Of course, the economic crisis stimulated negative survival responses in the form of a rise in crime and violence as the lumpen-proletariat expands with the deepening crisis. Illegal re-distribution of income comes into play as bank robberies, business payroll hijacks and housebreaking occurs. So the repressive arm of the state bears down heavily. Police brutality and army mobilization against the citizenry are features of the times. Police harassment is aimed particularly at those people with outward manifestations of the culture of Dread.

Mass organizations like trade unions and political parties are instruments for channeling the struggle of the people against imperialism. The two major trade unions in Jamaica are party unions, BITU with the JLP and NWU with the PNP. Accordingly, they operate within the two-party Westminster competitive political system. Together, they represent about 25% of the labour force.

Small independent unions have been increasing their membership by organizing high strata workers like clerks and supervisory staff (e.g. JALGO, UTASP); by organizing lower strata workers in small establishments and in workplaces where workers become dissatisfied with either or both of the big two party unions (e.g. DMWU, UAWU). The big two are joined in a struggle to keep down their smaller independent rivals. The railway dispute in late 1979 was one manifestation of this. And because of their structural connection with government, the executive arm of the state comes down heavily on the independent unions.

5. The Class Basis of Zig-Zag Politics

In order to understand the political process that accommodates the zig/zag character of the Manley regime we need an analysis of the structure of the PNP. Diagram 8.2 illustrates that in fact the articulation of the party comes from the charismatic leadership of Michael Manley at the top of the pyramid; and that social stratification within the party's decision making structure replicates the pattern of stratification in the society as a whole.

Casually-employed workers, small peasants, the unemployed and lumpen proletariat who are the majority in the mass base of the party have restricted access to upward mobility in the party structure. The same is true of women who are the main party workers and organizers — at the grass roots level. In between electoral campaign periods, it is the women who keep the party machinery in motion. And they are the hardest-campaigners as well in the electoral contests. Yet women are not visible in the decision-making hierarchy. One woman got elected as an officer of the Party in 1979 and there are only *three* among the forty members of the Executive.

It is important to note that whereas the PNP had 2,000 party groups in 1976 only about 500 existed by mid-1979. This is yet another index of the erosion of the social base after Manley abandoned his call for socialist self-reliance and embarked on the capitalist IMF road.

After mid-1979 Manley shifted again to the left. It had become clear that the economy could not adjust to the IMF medicine and that by December 1979, it would be necessary to seek extra accommodation from the Fund. Meanwhile the rank and file of the party began to articulate a demand for the return of the leftist General Secretary, D.K. Duncan, who had been dismissed in 1977. The party reinstated Duncan at the September Annual Conference and Manley made a militant anti-imperialist presentation to the Non-Aligned Conference in Havana.

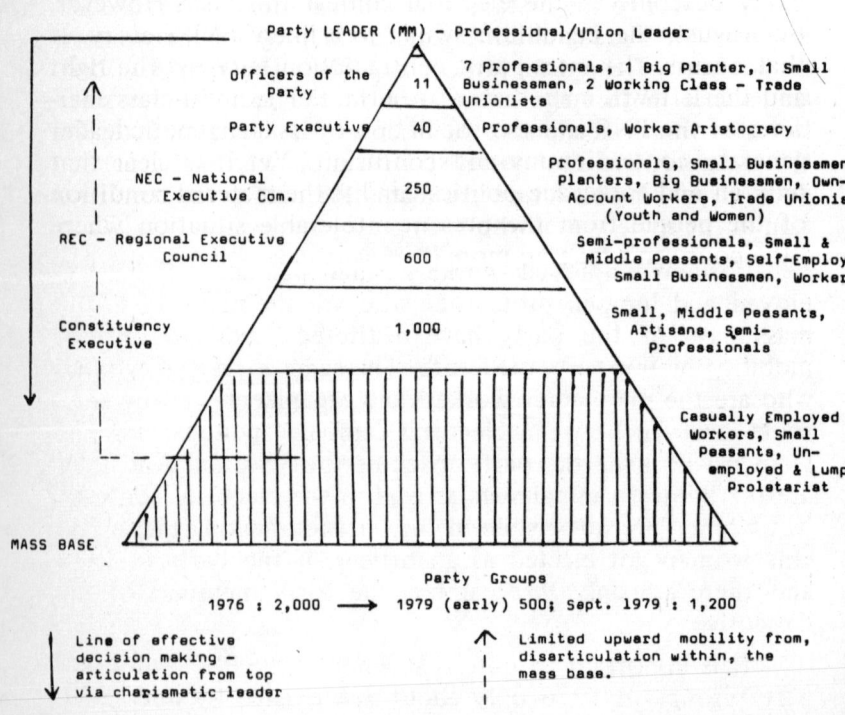

Diagram 8.2

As expected, government failed the December 1979 IMF test. And in January 1980 the question of a non-capitalist (anti-IMF) alternative was placed firmly on the agenda by rank and file party delegates at a Special Delegates Conference of 2,500 held January 13, 1980. As Manley said himself in his closing address to that meeting "the intellectual capacity of the people has been honed by adversity" generated by the IMF path. On March 22, 1980, the National Executive of the Party voted 2 to 1 for government to break with the IMF. Cabinet took that decision at its next meeting the following week even though the majority of them (all except two) had voted otherwise at the NEC meeting. Opposition to the non-capitalist path is as strong inside the Cabinet as it is among the opposition JLP and the reactionary class of bourgeois and petit-bourgeois elements of Jamaican society.

In January 1980 the balance of forces in the national polity favoured the right and a JLP victory was then the most likely outcome of the electoral contest this year. However, by August, the pendulum swung to a likely PNP victory. If that occurs, the intra-party contradiction between the right and the left will immediately re-surface. The multi-class character of the PNP and the vacillation of its charismatic leader generate contradictions and confusion. Yet it is clear that only an end to zig-zag politics can lift the material condition of the people from the present intolerable situation where "the poor can't take no more"!

CHAPTER 9

THE STRUGGLE AHEAD — THE 1980's

1. Some Economic Facts on the
   Future of the Economy

Population projections prepared for the Five Year Development Plan, updated, estimate that between 1980 and 1990, Jamaica's population will grow by about 263,000 people. That is *after* taking account of falling birth rates, and emigration of *10,000* people a year.

Education: The population of school age will grow by 100,000 to 270,000 in 1990. The additional school places required would be 65,000, which could cost anywhere between $65 million and $260 million in 1979 dollars, depending on how they are built.

Housing: The estimated requirement of 22,800 conventional units a year would cost $524 million a year in 1979 dollars. In 1979 expenditure on new housing is running at about $150 million.

Urbanisation: In 1990 about 1.3 million people will live in urban areas, 300,000 more than now, 53% of the total population. The cost of urban services is rising.

Food: About 70% of the population is below the recommended daily allowance of nutrition. Our food consumption should be about $1,444 million, $531 million more than in 1978. If food prices grow at 5% a year by 1990 our food requirement will be nearly $3,000 million. The recent World Bank report points to the possibility of serious world food shortages in the 1980's. The country that cannot feed itself will either starve or be on international welfare.

Energy: Projections of a year ago estimated that we would be spending at least US$1,100 million on energy imports in 1990, and possibly $2,100 million, US$800 - $1,800 million more than in 1978. But since then energy prices have gone up by 50% in six months. The country that cannot provide for energy will be condemned to perpetual stagnation and poverty.

Employment: The labour force will grow by about 315,000. To reduce unemployment to 10% by 1990 will require

471,400 new jobs. The cost of a new job in industry is at least $30,000 in 1979 dollars. If even one-third is provided by industry, leaving the rest to be provided by agriculture and services, the investment cost would be $466 million a year. In *1978* the total investment in Jamaica was $485 million.

International Conditions

(i) Trade: The *World Development Report* of the World Bank for *1978* tells us that growth rates have slowed down in the world capitalist economy, and are likely to remain very slow throughout the 1980's: GNP of developed capitalist countries: *one-third* slower in 70's than 60's 3.4% compared to 4.9%; growth rate of world trade: *4% 1973-77,* compared to 9% 1965-73; growth rate of developing country exports: *3.6% 1973-77,* compared to 6.4%.

Now a deep recession is beginning to take place in the U.S. economy. The OECD is predicting 0-1% growth rate in the developed countries for 1980. Trade restrictions in the developing countries are also growing.

(ii) Investment: For investment, World Bank estimates that developing countries will need $283 billion a year capital flows by 1985. In 1976 it was only $62 billion a year.

To sum up, the picture for the decade of the 1980's is dread. The path forward is full of thorns, whichever road we take. Our society is at a cross-road today. The political choice we face is between a continuation of dependent capitalism on the one hand; and transformation to a path of self-reliant socialism, on the other.

From the analysis presented throughout this book the choice is clear. Only a socialist development path can eradicate existing gross economic disequalities and remove the social ugliness which now stands in contradiction with the physical beauty of our land. But the questions are: what kind of socialism? How can it be achieved? And at what cost to our society? The next two chapters explore these questions in a manner that is intended to bring the collective wisdom of our people to bear on what is required in the struggle ahead.

2. The Conjuncture at the Start of the 1980's

Traditional New Year festivities were marred with the thought that 1980 will be dreader than 1979. The messages of the leaders of the two contending political parties made this clear to the nation. The fact is that IMF-engineered imperialism and government compliance with that strategy had brought the economy to the "brink of disaster" by mid-January.

In order to carry on for the first quarter of the year foreign exchange requirements are of the order of US$286 million, of which $136 million is to provide imports needed to maintain consumption levels, and to bring in raw materials and capital goods to keep production going. Additionally, the IMF has demanded a cut of $300 million from government expenditure. This would necessitate massive lay-offs of some workers and severe cuts in social welfare programmes for the poorer classes.

The IMF holds the handle while government holds the blade. The first cut in July 1977 was not the deepest. The deepest cut comes *now* if government seeks a new "modified agreement", beginning with the grant of a waiver from the Fund for failing the December 1979 "IMF test". The alternative is to break with the IMF, reschedule foreign debts, seek material assistance from socialist countries of the CMEA group and the People's Republic of China, and bridging financial assistance from friendly OPEC states and the Eurodollar banking fraternity. The international capitalist MNB's do lend to socialist countries, once there is a clear line of policy and "bankable guarantees" for repayment. (For example, firm marketing contracts for projects which earn foreign exchange are bankable guarantees).

In the words of the Mighty Diamonds, in 1980, "it a go bitter" within the IMF trap. Signs of the politics of adversity are already in the air. The following is a sample of such activities:

    (i)   the recent rush of housewives on certain Kingston supermarkets that brought police intervention to close the doors;

    (ii)   customs clamp down on higglers involved in the 'Panama hustle' that prompted a demonstration by the higglers concerned;

(iii) the increase in mental illness among the poor as evidenced by the marked rise in the number of mentally unbalanced persons roaming the streets (cf. *Star,* Jan. 1980 for a report from Bellevue officials on their recent intake of such persons, and the heightening crisis of space at that hospital which, with 1,800 beds, is more than three times the size of each of the two city General Hospitals — KPH and UHWI).

(iv) rural road blocks around mid-island Mandeville in response to the new gas price increase;

(v) the JPSCO power strike of supervisory staff that cost millions of dollars of production to industry and untold suffering for households;

(vi) the Railway dispute which impairs the movement of poor people and of goods, especially bauxite/alumina. Foreign exchange losses from the resulting need of the bauxite companies to shift from rail to road transport are of the order of US$10 million.

(vii) the Nurses Association of Jamaica dispute which seriously jeopardizes the health of poor people;

(viii) the wildfire and wildcat nature of industrial disputes (the CMP workers holding managers hostage being a dramatic example) leading to work stoppages time after time;

(ix) incessant and daily grumblings of household managers (i.e. "housewives") concerning shortages of basic consumer items; and

(x) increased crime and violence related to survival (e.g. petty thefts of food from households).

A brief commentary and analysis of these manifestations of the politics of adversity is instructive of the inherent contradictions of the competitive Westminster political process; and of the contradictions of dependent capitalism.

Only item (iv) above perhaps reflects the machinations of the official Opposition tribal politics. Items (v) and (vi), and (vii) are a direct result of the hegemony of the two-party trade unions (NWU and BITU) which co-jointly, and *with government consent,* are on a campaign to beat down challenges from small independent unions (like DMWU, UTASP, etc.) that have been organizing certain neglected categories of workers. Item (viii) indicates that unionized workers are ahead of union bosses in making militant demands for a better share of the increased productivity of their labour; thereby to reduce the degree of exploitation exercised on them by the capitalist class. Unrest among teachers and civil servants reflect government budget constraints.

All the items listed above are rooted in the structural crisis of international capitalism; and exaggerated by the harsh constraints imposed on the economy by the IMF. It is by now crystal clear that a IMF-type solution has been and will be incapable of solving the crisis. And the majority of *poor* Jamaicans know this now. In the words of Prime Minister Manley "the intellectual capacity of our people has been honed by adversity" (cf. speech to PNP Special Delegates Conference, January 13, 1980). But the same cannot be said for the more privileged classes.

3. Polarization of Class Forces

The national bourgeois, petit-bourgeois and professional classes are of the view that the problem is simply one of government "mismanagement". And organizations representing these classes (PSOJ, JMA, Chamber of Commerce, and the *Daily Gleaner)* recently issued calls either for government resignation or formation of a caretaker "national unity" government made up of their "best brains". Their intention to subvert the will of the people met stout resistance from government.

And so the struggle continues: the capitalists holding the big stick of close down and lay-off of workers; the workers demanding their rightful share of the huge profits being made by the capitalists, but kept down by the IMF-imposed wage restraint in the context of escalating prices; small peasants desperately seeking more land while government Project Land Lease is slashed by IMF demands; the dispossessed classes cling on through hustle activities; and Government is caught in an untenable position of trying to reconcile these irreconcilable contradictions.

At this juncture, the polarization of class forces expressed within the nation as outlined above is reproduced within the ruling party itself. This is inevitable in a multi-class party operating within a bourgeois democratic political framework. In the preceding chapter we presented an analysis of the class structure of the PNP as well as a schematic outline of the national balance of political forces.

The critical factor at mid-January, 1980 is the affirmation of the potential power of the left wing of the ruling PNP and the extra-party left, especially the WPJ. The right wing of the PNP does *not* accept the mandate of the hard-core rank and file party membership to make a break from the IMF-led path. And the top state technocracy shares this view as well.

Once more, Prime Minister Manley is caught on the horns of a dilemma. How to heal the breach between the two wings of his party? To break or not to break with IMF-led imperialism? If he decides to break, how to mobilize the Jamaican population at a time when the majority are disaffected by the politics of adversity? If he decides not to break, how much more will the poor take before unleashing massive social protest of a kind that will force the security arm of the state into repressive action, thereby setting the stage for the emergence of fascism?

The Fascist style of Seaga-led opposition JLP is already poised to take office "by overthrow or underthrow". And an increasing number of the national bourgeoisie and petit-bourgeoisie are in support of that alternative. One critical question is what USA-led imperialism regards as the best option to preserve and secure their interests in Jamaica, the Caribbean and the world.

When we consider the U.S.A. response to progressive changes in Nicaragua and Grenada, their aborted attempt to isolate Cuba from the Non-Aligned Movement prior to the September 1979 Conference in Havana, the launching of a military "Caribbean Task Force"; when, further, we consider their slippage of control in Iran, Afghanistan, and the Middle East generally with its strategic oil supplies, the consequent military mobilization in that region and the establishment of 100,000 strong 'Alert Task Force' capable of engaging within 24 hours anywhere in the world; and when, lastly, we consider the pending defeat of imperialism by the Liberation forces of Southern Africa, it becomes clear that the back of imperialism is to the wall and that the situation regarding

Jamaica poses a real problem to them.

In these circumstances, we can only speculate on the question of what imperialism would find most desirable for them in the upcoming electoral contest in Jamaica. Assuming that the state administration of the U.S.A. have learnt the bitter lesson of supporting fascist regimes in Iran (the Shah), in Nicaragua (Samoza), in Chile (Pinochet), and in Grenada (Gairy), then at least their Department of State — though perhaps not the CIA — *should* be unwilling to encourage the emergence of fascism in Jamaica. But the behaviour of a cornered beast is notoriously fierce! And 1980 is Presidential electoral year in the U.S.A.

On the other hand, a Manley-led PNP administration seems undesirable because of the potential of revolutionary socialism arising from the upsurge of an incipient socialist force for which Michael Manley has provided a protective umbrella so far. The difficulty of Manley's choice is compounded by the contradiction of his internal and external postures and policies. What seems clear is that Manley's traditional balancing act can no longer succeed. Yet he must prepare to face an electoral contest this year (1980).

The critical conclusion we draw from this analysis is that party control over the PNP's left-wing, the imposed "critical support" policies of the WPJ/CPJ, and the "Maoist theology" of the YFNL, all serve to provide Manley with an opening to continue on the dependent underdevelopment IMF-sponsored capitalist path, provided he can secure a new "modified agreement" from the Fund and the financial backing of the Euro-dollar banking syndicate. This is indeed the position that Manley articulated at the 'historic' March NEC meeting. But he could not persuade the majority of members present away from their commitment to shift away from the IMF and imperialism.

The question remains as to what external supports the country can secure outside of the imperialist system. Hard currency assistance from the CMEA socialist bloc is a non-starter because bourgeois social democratic regimes, like the Manley government would use such funds to support capitalism internally and internationally. And sympathetic and "friendly" oil rich OPEC states are few in number and they have internal economic problems of their own associated with the crisis of world capitalism, and with the class divisions within their social structures. Such countries as Iraq, Lybia and Algeria and those of the CMEA group will require a positive sign of action from the Manley regime before committing substantial resource support. Breaking with the IMF and launching on a "non-capitalist" path is an important signal. But Jamaica's position on Israel and on Palestine liberation is also critical for support from the oil-rich states.

CHAPTER 10

SCENARIO FOR TRANSITION TO SOCIALISM

In this final chapter, we offer some proposals for change that could be achieved by the start of the 21st century. At that time babies born this year will be leaving the teenage stage. The youth of today will be approaching middle age. And the middle aged of today will retire from the labour force. Our older folk will have passed on, leaving a legacy of thought and struggle to guide us forward.

The struggle over the next two decades will be a struggle in which both class and race will figure prominently in order to eradicate the inequalities created by a legacy of capitalist underdevelopment. In our view, two decades is the minimum time for a sustained programme of political education to bear fruit, in terms of *uni-directional* transition.

1. The Political Economy of Transformation

The basic condition for a socialist path of self-reliant development is a transformation of the political and social environment to release the creative dynamic of the dispossessed masses of Afro-Jamaican people. Control of the material base of the economy must pass from foreign capitalists, from big local capitalists and from bureaucratic government officials to the people. A socialist path of self-reliance is impossible without a real transfer of power to the people. The social history we have outlined throughout this book clearly attests to the great potential of our people — our human resources.

When one compares Jamaica with other countries less well endowed with natural resources (e.g. Israel) it seems obvious that our natural resource base is more than sufficient to provide decent levels of living for the whole population. We suggest as well that sufficient financial capital can become available with internal structural and institutional re-organization, and external assistance in the form of fraternal co-operation with other Third World countries. And finally, we assert unequivocally that management is already in plentiful supply. Anybody who doubts the managerial capacities of Jamaicans need only ask themselves how in these times of severe hardship, poor people are able to find food for their children and shoes and bus fares to send them to school — surely a miracle of domestic household management.

These assertions are already boldly supported by the record of achievements in social history of Afro-Jamaican people. All that is required is people control of the material base of the society and the associated transformation of the social environment. It is with that view of change that we turn to examine the economic possibilities and to outline some structural adjustments that are necessary in order to achieve economic independence and social justice.

Even though we are concerned with the long term in looking over the economic horizon we offer certain concrete proposals relating to the medium-term. We begin with a clear statement of objectives. These are :

(i) eradication of mass poverty
(ii) creation of full employment
(iii) promotion of social equality
(iv) achievement of economic and political independence, and
(v) establishment of our integrity as a nation to reinforce our psychological independence.

In order to achieve these objectives the planning strategy must aim jointly to match resource availability to demand and to match demand to needs.

The distinction between demand and needs is a crucial one because much of the existing consumer demand has been conditioned and shaped by the dishonest advertising associated with our legacy of dependent capitalism. And there is a significant gap now between that demand and what is really required for the well-being of our people.

The other gap — that between resource availability and demand — is one created by the manner in which our economy was inserted into the international capitalist system, as already described in earlier chapters. Thus today, for the most part, we still produce what we do not consume and we consume what we do not produce.

The stated objectives and the planning strategy outlined above indicate the kind of product mix which the economy must be geared toward achieving. The production and fair distribution of basic needs for the whole population is the priority of the programme/plan. In concrete terms, this requires .

(1) Production and distribution of a supply of *food*, adequate to provide proper nourishment for all; thereby banishing the present plague of malnutrition existing among our people (especially young children and pregnant women) .

(2) production and distribution of adequate *shelter* for all. A massive low-cost house construction and repair programme is the priority here in order to improve the conditions of living of the poor;

(3) production and distribution of *clothing* adequate to the limited demand of our tropical environment at cost levels which even the lowest paid workers can afford is certainly within the capacity of our national resource availabilities;

(4) provision of adequate *health* facilities for all can be achieved partly through provision of basic needs (1), (2) and (3) above. For some of the diseases and ill-health which now afflict the poorer classes stem from shortages of food, shelter and, to a lesser extent, clothing (e.g. shoes to protect the feet from parasites). Additionally, mental disorders among the poor stem largely from the frustrations of being unable to secure the material needs of basic subsistence. But more specific provisions for improving the health of our people are needed as well. And we suggest that all the necessary facilities for appropriate, preventive and curative medicine can be provided with the resources and technology that are already available;

(5) provision of appropriate and adequate *education* for all our people is a necessary requirement for upgrading skills and technology to enhance production, and for our full development as human beings, as well. Indeed, as we will soon demonstrate below, emphasis on education is an urgent priority because of present widespread illiteracy, especially among the youth component of our labour force.

In the rest of this section we map out a programme to supply the five basic needs identified above. First, we outline possibilities for the next 3 - 5 years and, secondly, we present a scenario for 2000 A.D.

2. The Economic Horizon Just Ahead

In the previous chapter, we presented official projections for population growth and economic conditions for the 1980's decade. Here we now present a summary outline of what can be done immediately. Crisis needs are now greatest in regard to food, employment and education. Food shortages are acute; and food prices have increased more rapidly than other categories in the household expenditure basket in recent times. The official estimates of unemployment is 25% of total labour force. This unemployment is most acute for youth (14-29 years old) and women. Two-thirds of the youth in the labour force are unemployed; and three-quarters of women who want work cannot find employment.

As concerns education, the illiteracy problem is startling especially when we consider that it affects a large and growing share of the youth. According to government's *Five Year Plan, 1978-1982,* the estimate is 40% functional illiteracy for the population as a whole. But as Vaughan Lewis points out in a comment on the Plan, this situation will become more acute because of (i) the rising proportion of working-age youth in the total population (from 25% in 1975 to 32% in 1983). and (ii) "the fact that about 40% of those leaving the formal education system are still functionally illiterate", according to the Plan.

As Lewis emphasizes, the linked phenomenon of (a) the "rapidly expanding youth population, (b) lagging employment and ... declining employment prospects, and (c) the functional illiteracy rates constitute an area of extreme political and economic importance." For no country in the modern world can achieve economic development with a labour force lacking in basic skills of literacy (including numeracy).

Although placing primary focus on food, employment and education at this time, we do not mean to imply that health and clothing do not require immediate planning action as well. In the case of health, shortage of drugs and medical professionals (i.e. doctors, nurses, radiographers, etc.) is a pressing problem; as is the limited supply of clinics and the deteriorated state of hospitals. In the case of clothing, the chief immediate problems relate to the production of textiles by Ariguanabo Mills, children's school uniforms, and shoes for the poorer classes.

The general strategy we propose for producing the three categories of basic goods in adequate quantity and quality is the utilization of labour-intensive techniques, and the mobilization of artisan and community labour. Given the widespread unemployment noted above, production of sufficient food, housing and clothing can create sufficient jobs to reduce the level of unemployment to a more tolerable situation. This can be achieved at much lower costs than the *official* estimates given in the last chapter if 'intermediate technology' rooted in the cultural traditions of the folk is employed.

For example, non-wage labour exchanges among communities of poor people in food production and house construction are part of the historical tradition of the development of the peasantry in rural areas and of the 'displaced peasantry' in town and city communities. When we consider that labour costs in house building are some 60% of the cost of construction, the savings implications for *low-cost* housing would be tremendous.

In the area of food production, the same principle of community mobilization of non-wage labour ("morning sport" and "day-for-day") can be re-introduced on a scale that would permit rapid expansion of food production, as well as capital improvements, like terracing and drainage on individual farms. Additionally, community production infrastructure, like irrigation works, could be developed on a rapid scale.

Finally, the clothing problem can be tackled effectively by allocating textile output of the Ariguanabo Mill through a state-parish-community distribution system to co-operative and community artisan producers (CEO's, etc.) in order to supply, in order of priority : (1) school uniforms, (2) other uniforms, (3) clothing for farmers, mechanics, etc., and (4) the indigent and poor who can be integrated in a skill improvement programme by apprentice employment.

For the basic social services — health and education — the strategy we propose involves a national labour mobilizational campaign to rapidly expand construction of clinics, polyclinics, and basic schools. The state-owned Cement Company and State Trading Corporation (STC) importers of building supplies should give priority to these community-organized construction activities at a price lower than cost. This subsidy can be recouped by a differential pricing system, whereby big capitalist firms (like WIHC) producing houses for the lower and upper middle class pay a slightly higher than normal price.

The critical factor for both health and education however, is more in the matter of personnel, technology and direction. Para-medical technology which integrates 'traditional' folk medicine with 'modern' medical achievements is the key for both preventive and curative medicine. What needs recognition and emphasis is that both the 'traditional' and the 'modern' are *scientific.* In child delivery, the skills of our traditional midwives are well recognized. But much more recognition and research is required concerning bush medicines for indigenous production of drugs; and in folk psychiatry — i.e. the balm-yard healer and obeah man.

The battle for eradicating functional illiteracy, in our view, is so urgent that consideration should be given to closing the U.W.I. for one academic year; and diverting student and staff activity to a national campaign. U.W.I. teachers' attention should be directed to research in appropriate technology requirements and relevant textbook writing in the interim. Additionally, the summer vacation should be used to bring high school student brigades to join the campaign. In this connection, the urban to rural (and vice versa) movement would benefit the student-teachers whose knowledge of Jamaica's natural environment would be enhanced immeasurably. High school teachers accompanying these brigades can help their students by linking practical exposure to plant and animal life with the theoretical knowledge they now impart. In the process, appropriate school textbook materials for primary and secondary levels can be produced.

C.A.S.T., J.S.A., Teachers Training Colleges and the Technical High Schools (including the Jose Marti Secondary) should not be disturbed in this interim national crash campaign relating to education. Indeed some U.W.I. teaching and research resources should be re-directed to these institutions because in the longer term scenario we present below, this is a requirement for meaningful and productive socialist transformation.

In rounding off this discussion of the economic horizon ahead, we turn attention to the question of administrative organization and management as well as the matter of political mobilization.

It is patently obvious that a clear socialist ideological line is essential for political mobilization of a kind that can promote and sustain this medium-term transition programme. The question that arises is : what political organization within the body politic at present are capable of providing this line? The answer emerging, from our earlier analysis, is *none*. What is required, therefore, is the promotion of an alliance of "socialist" forces which will begin to develop and activate an indigenously-rooted ideological framework for advancing the struggle ahead, in a manner that finds an articulation of theory and praxis which will trigger a responsive chord in the collective mind of the masses of black Jamaican people from which the professional class and the intelligentsia emerged only recently.

Lastly, on the question of organization and management it is clear that the present neo-colonial bureaucratic state apparatus must be dismantled. The replacement system must be people and community based. That is the crown-to-people Westminster system of welfare dispensation in the service of imperialism must be transformed to a People's Power system rooted in the Jamaican experience.

3. Outlines of a Social Framework

As a start in this exercise, we present a brief analysis and a set of proposals. Jamaican society is structured in the following manner :

(1) At the base is the household-family which includes members of an extended family (household head being male or female, plus children of all types of male/female sexual relations, plus grannie, auntie, etc.).

(2) The composition of households within a certain geographical space constitute a *village* in rural areas

and *neighbourhood/corner* in urban areas. At this level people meet face to face on a daily basis.

(3) A cluster of villages make up a rural *district* or a cluster of neighbourhoods an urban *community*. At this level, certain administrative institutions exist — e.g. post office, police station, public market, shops and commercial, industrial and banking activities. Face-to-face people relations here are more on a weekly basis.

(4) Several district/communities then constitute a *parish*. The parish is the headquarters of local government administration, e.g. Tax Office, Court House, and central government sub-units like P.W.D. Additionally, the parish capital has a general hospital, high schools, large commercial and industrial activities, and a large public market. Household heads visit the parish capital weekly (higglers, etc.) or monthly (e.g. teachers) and annually (e.g. to pay taxes).

(5) The *nation* is the aggregation of all the preceding levels and is administered by Central Government.

But, as already demonstrated in Chapter 8, the neo-colonial nature of the state apparatus is an obstacle to possibilities for transformation since it is the broker mechanism for imperialism's oppression and exploitation of the people. At present, local government in Jamaica is underdeveloped because of the disarticulation inherent in peripheral capitalism. Local government authorities (KSAC and Parish Councils) have been appropriately described as "expenditure committees of central government".

The introduction to the Five-Year Plan provides a succinct description of the disjointed character of state administration. Four components of the state act more or less independently of each other:

(i) Central government ministries and departments,
(ii) Local government authorities,
(iii) Statutory boards, and
(iv) State enterprises.

With no central co-ordination and planning there is inevitable waste and overlap. For example, in Kingston quite frequently the same street is dug up successively by the Water Commission, the Telephone Company, and the KSAC in three separate operations. And prime agricultural land which might be earmarked by the Ministry of Agriculture for food production may be under the control of the Housing Ministry or the Urban Development Corporation.

Clearly there is need for centralized *planning*. But at the same time there is need for de-centralization of political power and decision making in order to involve people in the political process. People outside of Kingston are alienated by the fact that all decisions affecting their lives are made in Kingston. And even within the city there is no scope for popular participation. A handful of individuals in big business and the state (some in both arenas at the same time) are in control. In the same way that economic power is concentrated among a few, so also is political power.

A socialist path of development involves real economic and political democracy. That is to say the productive resources of the society must be owned and controlled by the masses of workers and peasants. To translate this ideal in practice, it is necessary to introduce institutions for collective economic activity and to develop an administrative apparatus that anchors the political process in community based government.

Co-operatives and Community Enterprise Organizations (CEO's) are two organizational structures that should be expanded on a national scale to give economic power to the people. Ever since enslavement in Africa, co-operative activity has been the cornerstone of the resistant struggles of Afro-Jamaican people. And the success of the sugar co-operatives under the most unfavourable of conditions in recent years demonstrate the viability of this type of economic organization. CEO's are a recent (1978) innovation for community ownership and control of business activity. The Act which gives legal status to community councils widens the scope for a national programme of development of CEO's.

Operationally, rural CEO's should be land based institutions which incorporate economic activity in the production of food, housing, agro-industry, recreation (including tourism), and social infrastructure. Community councils would exercise direct control over the development of these enterprises, through a management committee (or board of directors) while paid managers would look after the day-to-day operations. In this manner, community councils would be in a position to appropriate part of the surpluses generated for investment in social infrastructure for the benefit of the whole community.

Now economies of scale, technical complexity and market situation in certain activities dictate that only the state can own and control them. Heavy industries like bauxite/alumina, power generation; utilities like water, telephone and urban transport and services like air and maritime transport, and commercial banking and insurance require central organization by the state. Private enterprise can continue to function in traditional activities except for the distribution of basic goods. In order to ensure equitable distribution and control over prices such goods must move through a state-local government institutional network.

At the other end of the spectrum, we find that, normally, the village is too small in population to undertake large-scale enterprises. Accordingly, co-operatives are an appropriate type of economic organization at that level. Moving up the scale, the district (and division) in most cases are large enough to accommodate Community Enterprise Organizations. Diagram 10.1 provides an outline of the structural framework envisaged.

In this framework, local government begins at the village level where an elected council would preside over whatever co-operative productive activity is introduced and promote the welfare of the village/neighbourhood community. Delegates from each village/neighbourhood would be elected to serve on the district/community council . and, in turn, representatives from this level would constitute the parish council. Provision must be made for recall of non-performing elected officials. Parish councils should have revenue collecting powers to provide them with an expenditure base independent of central government. Property taxes, for example, should accrue to parish councils.

Now present *PARISH* boundaries are a reflection of a plantation past. Jamaica needs to be re-zoned into parishes that homogenize population and the resource base. Thus, for example, East St. Mary, Portland, and East St. Thomas share

PROPOSED ADMINISTRATIVE AND PRODUCTIVE ORGANIZATION
FOR SOCIALIST TRANSFORMATION

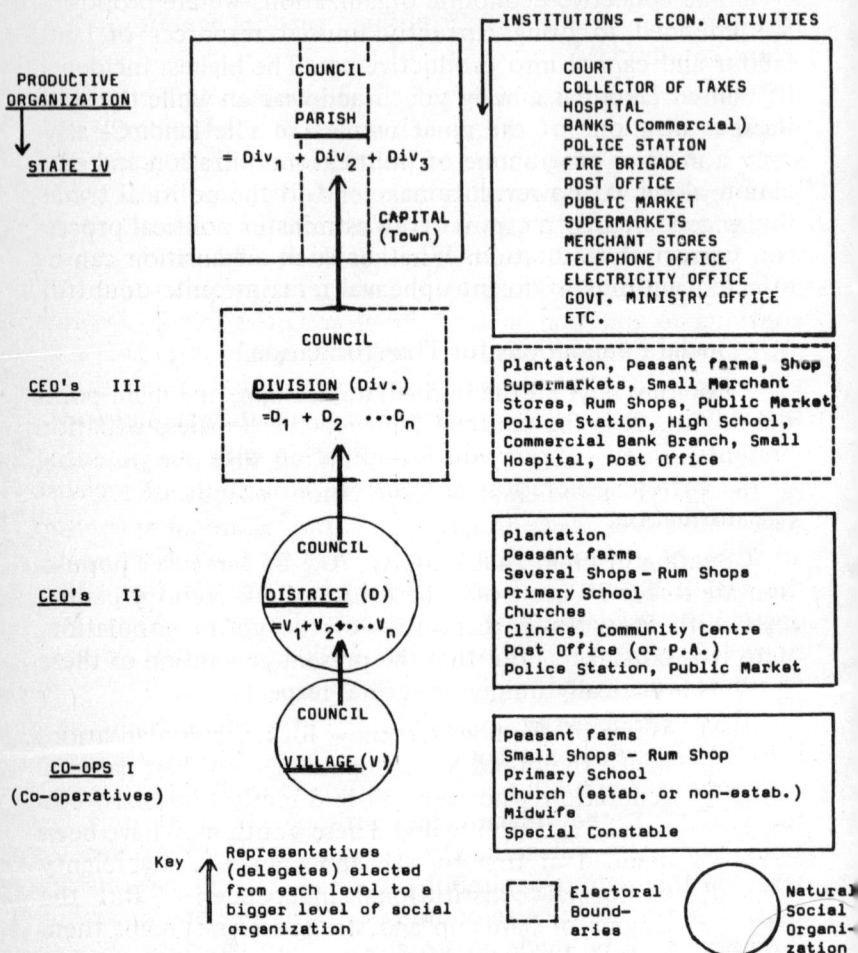

Diagram 10.1

common features in the concentration of banana-coconut production because of the homogenous ecological environment. Administratively, they could form one parish with research and developmental institutions relating to those two main crops located within that new parish. And so on, for other areas in sugar, bauxite, tourism, etc. A good deal of imagination in physical planning and social engineering is required in this exercise. And preparatory studies should begin right away. This is a longer term proposal.

The collective economic organizations we are proposing are intended to bring currently unused resources of land, labour and capital into productive use. The highest incidence of unused labour is among youth and women while the state itself is now one of the chief owners of idle land. Clearly, only a massive programme of political mobilization and education along with a revolutionary end to the political tribalism engendered by a two-party Westminster political process can correct this situation. Whether such a transition can be effected without a violent upheaval remains quite doubtful.

4. Social Foundations for Transformation

Looking beyond the immediate horizon, one main point stands out. It is the contrast between the hopeless situation presently faced by our youth population with the potential of the current generation of youth to contribute to socialist transformation.

Bearing in mind that close to 70% of Jamaica's population are under 29 years old, the future of our country plainly rests with the creative capacities of the youth population. Here it is crucial to note that the present generation of these youth is historically unique in several respects :

(1) Many of them never knew formal colonialisation, hence they tend to be impatient with their parents' generation who were more directly brutalized culturally and politically. These youth may have been deluded at first by the appearance of sovereignty of formal constitutional independence. But the lessons of hardship and struggle soon taught them to look beneath the surface of reality at the underlying dependent economic relations in which their country is trapped.

(2) For a number of reasons, this is the most conscious and skilled generation to emerge in this (and other Third World) country. Since World War II there has been tremendous growth in the technology of communication which has brought societies into closer contact with each other. In addition, this has been

the era of national liberation movements and the growth of socialism on a world scale. These youths therefore have been socialised in a world that is not only growing smaller, but one in which the masses of poor countries and their peoples have been asserting themselves evermore vigorously.

(3) With the improvements in the availability of education and of reading material generally, young people today are in every way better informed than used to be the case.

(4) While this generation has been subjected to illusions and false hopes stimulated by the distractions and opportunities for escapism through commercial advertisement, professional sports, drugs, etc., and generally increased exposure to the way of life in the advanced capitalist countries (principally those of North America), the very failure of their unrealistic expectations to materialize has resulted in a rising level of frustration and impatience with the glaring injustices and inequalities of class privilege in present day Jamaica.

When assessed against the potential contribution of the youth to the construction of the national economy, the situation of unemployment and the daily abuse of the body, mind and spirit are clearly a tragic waste of nature's greatest gift to our country: its young lives. As conscious and skilled workers, the youth represent the dynamic core of social instability. Presently, their alienation takes its daily toll in physical deterioration, mental illness, habits of criminality, drug addiction and loss of hope. Only a radical transformation of the present class structures of this country can release and mobilize the intelligence, the energy and the resourcefulness of the youth for constructive activity; to release our young people from the struggle for survival by hustle and crime to enable them to claim their birthright to a full human development.

It is in this dilemma that the scenario for the next two decades must address directly. Clearly, the political economy of transformation must be anchored on a philosophical (ideological) foundation that will rehabilitate the collective integrity of our people to produce Integral Man. We define the creation of 'integral man' as the challenging process of pulling together the pieces of alienated man into the opposite – i.e. a coherently articulated integral man and society.

That fundamentally is the task we face as a people. But how to achieve that goal? The answer to that must be to find a common chord to bind different classes in the struggle ahead. All social change involves sacrifice, but eventually all of our people must make some contribution to society. A socialist society has no place for parasites, but holds all who work, whatever their occupation, in equal respect.

The articulation of socio-economic order which depends on cementing a worker-peasant alliance to administer and direct the society's resources demands critical inputs from the professional and technical strata of the middle class, the state bureaucracy, and the "patriotic" capitalist class. It can be safely assumed that once foreign capital is driven out, a large part of the comprador capitalists (i.e. big national capitalists) will depart.

But the small business strata is more likely to choose, for patriotic reasons, to remain. This strata could come into its own, using appropriate technology to (i) utilize domestic raw materials, (ii) upgrade their innovational skills and that of workers involved and (iii) help to democratise the organization of production. Our earlier analysis indicated how the irrationality of small business production at present reflects the irrationality of government policies. With the kind of socialist transformation which is here proposed, the national importance of the "small business" capitalist class would be greatly enhanced.

Professionals, and the technical and administrative strata of the middle class will be needed to provide technical and managerial (e.g. accounting) expertise in the transformation process. And this contribution would naturally increase their *sense of importance* to the process of national building.

These kinds of benefits which the privileged classes will gain in the transformation process for raising the material and spiritual welfare of the dispossessed workers and small peasants must be balanced against the present high costs involved in personal and property security inherent in the system of dependent capitalism. (The sum of expenditures on grill works for houses and business places, special private security forces, guard dogs, etc., must be quite substantial in the present contextual situation).

The final consideration really synthesizes all the elements of disarticulation/disconnection/disjointedness in all aspects of our deformed peripheral capitalist economy and society. The indicative 20-year programme must be designed to correct the full set of contradictions. In the area of material production and distribution; in the area of state administration (including security to protect national sovereignty); and in the vital area of cultural development to eradicate the legacy of cultural imperialism and release the creative dynamic of our people. This creativity is evident in the cultural revolution already in train. The political revolution urgently needs to catch up with that process. Then, and only then, can the process of socialist transformation in Jamaica shift into high gear. Then, and not until then, will we as a people be able to reap sweet fruit from the sacrifices and hardships which we, as a people, have suffered during the initial and hesitating steps that have been taken in the direction of socialism in recent years.

EPILOGUE

Eleven months after the defeat of Manley's PNP by Seaga's JLP in the elections of October 1980, we see a need to assess with the aid of hindsight, the reasons for the change of government, the immediate impact on the society and the implications for the people's struggles. These questions must be answered if the people are to be prepared to reap the political whirlwinds they have helped to sow.

1. The October 30 Election

For several reasons, this was the most important election to date in Jamaica's history. In the first place, the ideological differences between the PNP and the JLP had never been as sharp. The PNP promised to continue to build Democratic Socialism, to chart a path of economic development without the help of the IMF and to deepen democracy in the processes of decision-making. The JLP promised to restore the free enterprise system, to manage the state and the economy efficiently and to fight communism, all under the slogan of "Deliverance". (This term, as is so often the case in Jamaican politics, is a Biblical allusion promising to end the suffering that the people had endured in the previous 8 years).

Second, it was necessary for the society to make clear political decisions and settle down on some path of economic development if total collapse of the social order was to be avoided.

Third, it was the most violent. At least six hundred people lost their lives. Countless others were maimed or lost their houses and belongings. The technological level of warfare involved the most sophisticated and brutal terrorist techniques ever employed in Jamaica. One American organization estimated that over US$600,000 worth of automatic rifles — e.g. M-16 — had been brought into Jamaica, particularly from Miami. Further, the security forces (the army and the police) participated actively in all spheres of the election campaign, and particularly in the military sphere.

Fourth, it was the most expensive the society had ever held. Apart from the loss of life, the large-scale destruction of property and the campaign expenditures of both parties must have been phenomenal.

Several factors explain the defeat of the PNP, for the victory of the JLP must be seen largely as a repudiation of the PNP. First, the failure to come to grips with the economic crisis brought hardships to all strata of the society particularly the poor and the middle class. The JLP accused the PNP of economic mismanagement and the government's record of mistakes and failures made the charge plausible. In fact, much of the alleged mismanagement is endemic to the political system. The state still bears the character of the repressive colonial administration and as such is incapable of efficient management of resources for development projects. Further, it is rent and undermined by the sharp polarization of political tribalism. It is fair to say that the JLP's opposition strategy included the sabotage of state activities from within the state itself. In this regard, they were assisted by the internal divisions within the PNP itself.

Second, the PNP's close friendship with Cuba and the WPJ served to fuel the anti-communist campaign of the JLP. In the case of the Cubans, a series of incidents — the importation of hunting bullets for transshipment to Cuba through a dummy company, Moonex International; criticism of the JLP's anti-communist pro-imperialist posture by the Cuban Ambassador Estrada — were manipulated by the *Gleaner* to feed the JLP propaganda. In the case of the WPJ, an inordinately high profile in the campaign, albeit in support of the PNP, alienated traditional PNP right wing support, particularly in the middle classes. The anti-communist campaign also won the support of the reactionary political forces in the USA: the Reagan forces and the capitalists around him, and the Jamaican Community, particularly elements in the business community, which were self-exiled in the USA.

Third, the JLP were better organized. They had been campaigning since 1977, immediately after the 1976 elections. They had the resources of the entire Jamaican capitalist class, both those in the country and those in exile, as well as the resources of their American allies behind them. On the other hand, the PNP could only tap the resources of some of its friends in OPEC and an almost bankrupt State treasury. Thus the JLP could afford a massive media campaign and could afford to buy political support in the various ways characteristic of Jamaica's political culture. In addition, the PNP's campaign machinery was put into action late as the

Party Secretariat had been demobilized between the conferences of 1978 and 1979. Again this was a result of the internal struggle within the party.

Fourth, the institutions and organizations which exert power in the society had defected from the government and began to respond to the JLP. All the organizations of the business community — the Chamber of Commerce, the Jamaica Manufacturers Association, the Private Sector Organization of Jamaica — had become openly hostile to the government from the start of the second term. The JLP's union, the BITU, had grown stronger, (as is the usual case with opposition unions) under the PNP regime. Some of the professional organizations, reflecting middle class opinion were openly hostile to the government; others at least withdrew their support and trumpeted the criticisms from their special interests.

Sections of the religious establishment openly supported the JLP or at least echoed and endorsed the most vulgar anti-communism. In this regard, the Evangelicals were most hostile to the government. Beginning in 1977, there was a tremendous growth in Evangelism, especially at the expense of the indigenous Rastafari movement. The government paid scant attention to the reports that agents of destabilization, particularly the CIA, used the movement as a cover for their activities. There was support from the established churches as well for the JLP. So much so in fact that the Jamaica Council of Churches was denounced for not joining the chorus of anti-government criticism.

The campaign sharpened the polarization of the media. Two of the most powerful organs — the *Gleaner* and Radio Jamaica — had carried the anti-government campaign during the PNP's second term. The *Gleaner* in fact provided ideological leadership and, according to the Press Association of Jamaica, was an all too willing handmaiden for the CIA destabilization strategy. The JBC and the *Daily News* rallied more firmly behind the government as the election drew closer. In the end this might have even hurt the PNP, as it was taken to mean government manipulation of the media.

Finally, the organs of state power also deserted the government. Frustration among civil servants had been mobilized by the Civil Service Association into a strike in 1979. This organization became increasingly hostile to the government. More than that, some senior civil servants were thoroughly disloyal and sought to embarrass the government by sabotaging programmes and feeding information to the opposition JLP. Throughout 1980, there was paralysis throughout the state sector as people awaited the elections. For by then, unable to check the economic decline and the wave of terrorist violence, the PNP government had lost the moral authority to govern.

Sections of the judiciary were known to be openly anti-government. On the other hand the pro-government elements were circumspect in their support.

Crucially crucial was the role of the security forces. In the highly charged political atmosphere which pervaded the entire society, it was impossible for the security forces not to be politicized as well. Elements of the forces — police and soldiers — lined up on both sides, both in their official and private capacities. As it turned out, the security forces lined up overwhelmingly behind the JLP. The PNP's own analysis of their defeat identifies intimidation of their organizers and their voters by elements of the security forces as a principal factor.

In a real sense, then, there had been a process of transfer of power from the PNP to the JLP prior to the elections. The process began early in the PNP's second term and accelerated sharply in the final months. The organs of power — private and public — increasingly ignored the directives of the PNP government and responded deliberately, or by default, to the JLP. The election was then a sanction for this transfer of power.

While this was a free election, it was not completely fair. The reports of corruption and other election irregularities were too numerous to be discounted. And even if the JLP manipulated the election machinery better than the PNP, this was not the decisive factor. There was a massive voter turnout despite the military intimidation of PNP communities and supporters. The people voted out the PNP out of frustrations and hardships brought on by the economic crisis. They had grown weary of the terrorism — of wanton murder and burnings, a terrorism which defied explanation and violated their humanity. They were confused by the indecisiveness and zig-zag of the PNP government. Though their consciousness had been raised in the struggles of the 1970's, it was not raised sufficiently to avoid seduction by the JLP's promises, especially as food supply was short. The JLP promised prosperity ('money jingling in your pocket') and security. This is what the PNP had failed to achieve in 2 terms of office and their campaign — poorly financed, poorly organized and too short gave no reason to believe the third term would be any different.

2. The New Regime

The JLP government is an alliance of two main factions. The dominant faction led by Seaga, brings together big capitalists and landlords with a hard-core of urban unemployed and unemployables. This is an alliance reminiscent of plantation-type relations. Also in the Seaga faction are the more conservative elements of the brown middle class traditionally loyal to the PNP. The other faction, led by Shearer, consists of BITU workers and traditional peasant support loyal to the legacy of Bustamante.

The alliance contains a fundamental contradiction of class/race interests. The Shearer faction, drawing its support primarily from black working people, tends to be nationalistic. The Seaga faction, drawing its support primarily from white and socially white propertied people, tends to be pro-imperialist. On several occasions the contradictions arising from opposing class/race interests have rent the JLP. In 1978, Seaga offered his resignation as leader in an impasse with the Shearer forces. Since the election, new strains have developed over the government's anti-worker policies. Shearer in fact, appears to be using his position as Foreign Minister to push his own policies on issues affecting the Third World and on South Africa. This undoubtedly embarrasses Seaga's strong pro-USA stance.

The alliance of the two forces projects a populist image — however reactionary — with barely disguised fascist tendencies. It appealed to a broad cross-section of the electorate. The JLP in fact won the support of the majority of every social class and grouping. The big capitalists and landlords were implacably hostile to the PNP and openly loyal to the JLP during the entire second term of the PNP government. The burden of taxes, the uncertainties of employment and income and the hardship of shortages of basic goods and services alienated all but the most nationalistic elements of the middle classes. Even the workers and peasants who benefited most from the reforms of the PNP defected or remained aloof from the PNP. For they also suffered most from the rising cost of living, unemployment and uncertain employment. The youth were seduced by the JLP with cash, cheap but scarce imported consumer goods and political circus. In short, the JLP won a truly popular mandate in so far as it drew its support from the entire social spectrum.

But in particular it drew the support of the most reactionary sections of the propertied classes. Many of them had gone into self exile in North America, particularly Miami. Like a Trojan horse, they lodged themselves within the populist reaction donning the garbs of popular dissent. Here was the last chance to recapture power, restore themselves to the top of the social order and recapture their private preserve for exploitation, the Jamaican working people.

The Jamaican Community overseas, particularly in Miami, were both victims and purveyors of anti-government propaganda. These communities had grown rapidly as a result of the middle and upper class migration of the 70's. Many of them remained adrift in American society. Where they were rich, well-to-do, powerful or even influential in Jamaica, they were at best affluent nobodies in Miami. Where they were socially white, first class citizens in Jamaica, they were brown and black second class citizens in the USA. In their anger and frustration, they embraced the most backward political positions and allied themselves with the most racist and reactionary political forces in the U.S.A. − e.g. The John Birch Society. Miami is a confluence of reactionary exiles cast off by progressive and revolutionary social change in Latin America. There, the most reactionary elements of the Jamaican community struck anti-communist alliances with the likes of the Cuban gusano community which is the most active and militant agent of CIA destabilization in the region.

With the array of political forces mobilized by the JLP, the profile of leading personalities in the new regime was not surprising. Seaga is Prime Minister, Minister of Defence, Minister of Information and Culture and Minister of Mining and Energy. In other words, he alone is responsible for the State's money, guns and information, apart from the Prime Ministerial responsibilities of policy making.

Shearer is the Foreign Minister. As a black man, he projects a more appropriate image for the foreign minister of a black country. The responsibilities of foreign minister also distances him from the Union movement. Pernell Charles, another black man, is the Minister of Local Government, with responsibilities that require interfacing with the mass of poor people. The Minister of Industry and Commerce is Douglas Vaz, a socially white manufacturer who until recently was one of the leading personalities in the Seaga faction. The rest of the cabinet are drawn from the black and brown middle class and tend to be of marginal political significance, as far as leadership is concerned.

But the regime is broader than the cabinet. It includes other important public offices such as mayors, and heads of government agencies and companies. Many of these — and indeed the most powerful — are businessmen and professionals from ethnic minority groupings, those we have called socially white. The stark reality is that in a country that is 98% African of various hues, the Prime Minister, the Head of the Appeal Court, the Head of the Army and several major public figures (e.g. Mayor of Kingston, head of the Jamaica component of the joint US-Jamaica Private Sector Committee) are all socially white from the propertied elite.

3. The New Development Path

In their election campaign, the JLP had promised a new path for economic development under the politically loaded slogan of "freeing up" the economy. The slogan implies that there had been excessive regulation and control of the economy. In the context of the anti-communist campaign themes, the slogan appealed to those who feared, however spuriously, the alleged drift to totalitarian policies by the previous government.

The new path has three essential components:
(a) orientation of the economy toward export production
(b) industrialization by invitation
(c) unfettered rule of the market.

Historically, the economy had always been export oriented. Further, under the previous government, export production was also given pride of place in government policy, particularly in the allocation of foreign exchange and in the provision of incentives. But it was now to receive increased emphasis, even at the expense of production for the domestic market.

In order to expand production, particularly for export, foreign investors were to be extended virtually open invitations and wooed by incentives, so generous as to call into question the sovereignty of the nation. Existing incentive legislation already made generous concessions to foreign investors. But in addition, the government adopted postures to instill confidence in foreign investors in the Jamaican economy. For example, in an address to Canadian business interests, the foreign minister assured them that they would be free to repatriate their profits as they wished. The cornerstone of foreign policy, as we will see, has been to court a special friendship with the USA. On this path, the free play of market forces will dictate prices and the flow of economic resources to the various sectors of the economy. Under the whip of market competition, firms will be forced to be efficient while being free to make as much profit as the market will bear. These profits will finance subsequent expansion with the concurrent expansion of employment and the utilization of other resources.

This path is referred to by several names. The most common name is the "Puerto Rican Model" after the historically famous precedent originally called Operation Bootstrap. It is also called the "Taiwan Model" and the "Singapore Model" after two contemporary versions which have successfully maintained high growth rates in the last 10 years. But it could just have been called the "Jamaican Neocolonial Model". For all governments between 1955-1974 pursued this path and the associated policies with conviction. Between 1974-1978, the force of historical circumstances — in particular economic crises in its national and international aspects — prompted the government to consider an alternative path. While the government did so, perhaps by force of habit or perhaps by a momentum gathered over the past 20 years, the state continued to implement and support the old policies. To that extent the economy remained on the same old path. It had stalled — and even started to reverse! — and there was no longer official government conviction in this path. In a real sense, then, the new path chosen by the JLP is really the same old path. Only now they bring to it a sense of purpose and conviction matched only by the conviction of Reagan-Thatcher in Monetarist policies.

Upon assuming office, the new government concluded an Extended Fund Agreement with the IMF. Preliminary negotiation between the JLP and the IMF began months before the elections. This drew sharp criticism from the former Minister of Finance, as well as the late Prime Minister of Trinidad and Tobago, Eric Williams. The question was : was the IMF interfering in local affairs; more precisely, was the IMF interfering on behalf of the JLP and its forces?

a. The IMF Agreement

All IMF agreements with Third World countries are designed to ensure that the borrowing country remains within the world capitalist economy. Its markets and resources must remain open to foreign entrepreneurs — in reality, capitalists from the advanced countries. The political and economic climate should be hospitable in order to attract and inspire confidence in foreign investors.

The agreement concluded by the new JLP government in April 1981 was essentially the same one rejected by the PNP government in 1980, although the terms were not quite as harsh as those offered to the PNP government. The agreement provided for a loan of US$600 million under the IMF's Extended Fund Facility. This was to be drawn down over a period of 3 years subject to an agreed schedule, periodic monitoring by the IMF and the passing of certain tests set by the IMF. The tests derived from conditions of the loan which essentially sought to :

(a) restrict and reduce the role of the State in the economy
(b) restrict the rate of increase of the real wage — the real wage had already been cut by 35% by devaluations of 1978
(c) restore the "free" market as the sole regulator of the economy
(d) ensure a hospitable investment climate for foreign capital.

The government's economic policy coincided with these goals. Ministry Paper No. 9 states that "The government recognizes that the private sector is the main engine of economic growth and increased production and that an environment must exist within which private initiative and entrepreneurship will prosper. Consequently steps will be taken to remove progressively all controls that inhibit such an environment". (Annex II p.5). This is the statement of the policy called "Deregulation" which principally consists of

(a) liberalization of price controls — out of 60 commodities under price control, 18 were removed completely, and 12 partially;
(b) liberalization of rent controls, with the government monitoring low-income rentals. The immediate result was a massive rise (100% increases were not uncommon) in rentals particularly for middle income housing and commercial buildings;
(c) liberalization of exchange controls by easing import restrictions and simplifying licensing procedures with a view to ultimately dismantling the system.

Deregulation basically means that the State ceases to regulate, to exercise controls over important markets for basic commodities, housing and foreign exchange. Apart from that, the government pledged to reduce State intervention in marketing by scaling down the activities of the State Trading Corporation (STC) and the Agriculture Commodity Boards. The STC had been a bone of contention between the previous government and the IMF from its establishment in 1977. Under the new government $140 million worth of trade in certain food items and building materials were handed back to the private sector. Several State companies are to be sold or leased to private investors, local and foreign. This is called Divestment and is the work of a committee headed by a big businessman. Again, this is another way to reduce the role of the state in the economy.

As with all IMF agreements, firm limits were placed on government expenditure and borrowing. Further, precise guidelines for monetary policy were stipulated in the agreement in the form of targets/tests. The immediate impact of the ceiling on expenditure was a freeze on employment in the

State sector. Subsequently, under the guise of "reorganization" of the Ministries, departments and agencies of the State, hundreds of workers were laid off. Similarly, the Youth Employment Programme and the Special Employment Programme were "reorganized" with over 10,000 people losing their jobs. In many cases, victimization of supporters of the former government, particularly communists, was blatant. The mood of the country permitted and even encouraged the anti-communist hysteria of the government spokesmen. The SEP was reorganized as the "Relief Employment Programme" (a poignantly paternalistic change of name) with rank and file supporters of the new government replacing many of the former workers.

With the restrictions on borrowing imposed by the IMF Agreement, the State had to curtail or shelve many capital development projects which have been in the pipeline for years. Under the agreement, the current account deficit, 5% of GDP in 1980/81, is to be converted to a surplus 1% of GDP, by the end of the second year, 1983/84. It is therefore necessary to increase State revenues which have grown slowly in the previous years. Three factors accounted for the previous government's inability to raise sufficient revenue. First the State inherited the colonial tax machinery. Over the years it became progressively more inefficient and never developed the capacity to collect taxes on a wide range of incomes — e.g. own account income, ganja income etc. Second, economic decline meant less income to tax. Third, tax evasion, avoidance and withholding became political virtues for a business community openly hostile to the PNP government and friendly with the opposition JLP. After elections, with the JLP in power, the State was able to collect much of this outstanding revenue.

The 1981/82 Budget contained no new taxes. However, a new tax system was to be put in place by October 1, 1981. This system would replace "frontier taxes" (basically customs duties) with "inland taxes" — basically, sales taxes. As of September 1, the precise mechanisms for this transition have not been made known.

The sum total of Deregulation, reduction in State Marketing, Divestment, and restricted expenditure and borrowing was the reduction of the role of the State in the economy. This was consistent with the view of the private sector as the "engine of growth". It was a sharp reversal of the trend towards state leadership of the economy which developed under the previous government and which was rationalized through the principles of Democratic Socialism.

The IMF Agreement — unlike the previous ones with the PNP government — did not impose a ceiling on wage increases. It allowed private enterprises to pay what they could afford. But it restricted public sector workers to 3 year contracts and marginal increases. Due to the resistance of the unions, the government conceded to the tradition of 2-year contracts — a hedge for workers against inflation. However, it imposed a $29 per week increase over 2 years for all public sector workers. This led to massive industrial unrest in the form of a 2 week strike by Junior Doctors and the virtual curtailment of public health services, strikes in the public utilities and disgruntlement and disaffection among civil service workers.

Nor did this agreement insist on devaluation of the currency. However, the government warned in the presentation of the agreement to the nation that if wages rose too fast, it would have to consider devaluation.

Deregulation meant that the "free" market reasserted itself as the regulator of economic life. The impact of this will be discussed below. But it was also a cornerstone element in creating a hospitable climate for foreign capital. Despite the previous government's efforts to attract foreign capital, the presence of state control, however minimal, helped to fuel massive propaganda that there was a threat to private property.

For the new government this is not a concession. It believes that the free play of market forces will stimulate economic growth and development. Further it recognizes and acquiesces to the dependence of the economy on foreign capital. Accordingly it has gone to great lengths to woo American capital by seeking a "special relationship" with the US government as Reagan's number one Caribbean ally.

The IMF Agreement is accompanied by a programme of debt rescheduling agreed with Jamaica's major creditors. This eases the foreign exchange problem somewhat, but for a short while. The day of reckoning when the debts have to be paid must come. The IMF agreement will be reviewed in 1983/84 in the light of the government's progress in achieving the performance targets.

The IMF loan and the programme of debt rescheduling are two of the three prerequisites for the government to pursue its programme of economic recovery. The third component is the foreign investment which the government expects will drive the economy along the new/old path of (dependent capitalist) development.

b. International Relations

The new government successfully won the role of Reagan America's number one ally in the Caribbean and celebrated it with being the first foreign government leader to visit Reagan's White House. This was a cementing of alliances developed prior to the USA and Jamaica elections of late 1980. While in opposition the JLP had cultivated the friendship of right wing political and business organizations which formed the core of Reagan's support. The Secretary of the JLP openly declared his support for Reagan in a newspaper interview in the USA.

A common principle for both the JLP and its American allies is a crude anti-communism, that sees a Soviet conspiracy wherever people legitimately assert their rights and resist oppression and exploitation. The strong friendship between Manley's PNP government and the Cuban government had been the main fuel for the JLP's anti-communist campaign. Upon assuming office, Seaga's first act was to demand the recall of the Cuban Ambassador whom he accused of interfering in Jamaican affairs. Jamaica-Cuba relations were put in cold storage along with the technical assistance projects the Cubans had been engaged in. Over the years of the previous regime, Cuba and been generous in providing schools, "mini dams", doctors and training for Jamaicans in construction and other skills. All that remains is a low-profile presence of doctors who are not immediately replaceable. Ironically, the Cuban doctors were among the 10% who did not strike in April 1981.

Recently the Cubans have expressed the desire to normalize relations but so far the government of Jamaica has not responded. At the same time, Jamaica has been an outlet for Cuban refugees who are given visas to Jamaica even though they have no visa for their ultimate destinations. Ironically, there are probably more Cubans here now than under Manley. But whereas those who came in Manley's time were for the most part productive workers helping to build Jamaica, the Cuban refugees of today make no such contribution.

Apart from denouncing communism and sharply curtailing relations with Cuba to prove its mettle, the government has tended to line up behind the US in foreign policy. It declared that the El Salvador junta was a moderate government and even denounced France and Mexico for recognizing the leftist guerilla opposition to the junta. Relations with Haiti, South Korea and Taiwan have strengthened.

The only novel idea to come from the government to date has been the call for the Marshsll-type Plan for the Caribbean. Essentially the idea is that a massive programme of private investment and government aid should be mobilized to stimulate growth and employment in the region. Naturally the US would be the leader, but the plan includes participation by all the advanced countries. According to Seaga the Caribbean Basin Plan — the official name — requires US$3 billion of aid to the region; over what time period, he doesn't say. He projects that the shares of the donors will be :

Venezuela, Mexico, Trinidad and Tobago	$800m
USA	400m
Europe and Japan	300m
Multinational Institutions	200m

This is in addition to $1.3 billion in existing bilateral aid. The rationale for the Plan is that only by reducing the poverty of the region will the USA and its allies be able to ward off the spread of communism.

An institutional framework in the form of a joint committee of USA and Jamaican businessmen was established under the auspices of Reagan and Seaga. The USA Committee is headed by David Rockefeller of Chase Manhattan and Trilateral Commission fame. Also on the committee are several big businessmen whose corporations have interest in various sectors (e.g. energy (Exxon), Tourism (Hilton, Eastern Airlines), Mining (Alcoa)) of the Jamaican economy. The Chairman of the Jamaican counterpart is Carlton Alexander, perhaps the *de facto* leader of the local business community. With him are other big businessmen, one small businessman —

the only black businessman on the committee — and some of the government's top technocrats.

To date there have been several high-level meetings, and hundreds of million dollars of potential investment projects have been identified. Most of these have been in the State's pipeline for years, stalled for want of finance. But almost one year after the election there have been no major capital inflows arising out of the work of the committee. The Chairman of the US Committee Rockefeller even cautioned recently against unduly optimistic expectations about the speed and magnitude of foreign investment.

Similar joint committees are being established with Canada, Mexico and Venezuela, the other regional principals in the Caribbean Basin/Marshall Plan.

Within the Caribbean, Jamaica has assumed leadership of a pro-USA, anti-Cuban alliance along with Haiti, Barbados and some of the smaller countries. It has pledged its support for Caricom. But more than that, it wants to mobilize Caricom to press for and participate in the Caribbean Basin/ Marshall Plan. In its capacity as chief USA ally, it also participates in the regional hostility to, and political isolation of, the Grenada revolution.

So far, the only major difference that has arisen between USA and Jamaica foreign policy is over the South African invasion of Angola. The Jamaican foreign minister, Shearer, denounced South Africa. What is also instructive is that it probably reflects the contradictions between Shearer and Seaga on some issues. Shearer has been allowed to run his own foreign policy and has kept close to many of the positions of the former government on matters affecting Third World countries. Seaga, on the other hand, courts the North American businessmen and political leaders. The net effect, however, is a firm alignment with USA foreign policy unlike the previous government which zig-zagged from time to time in the name of non-alignment.

The new government is throwing the doors wide open to foreign investment. It is expected that North American capital, Jamaican capital spirited out in the 70's, and displaced capital from the El Salvadors and Nicaraguas of the region will be attracted to Jamaica. One set of consequences of this kind of policy will be .

(a) the reinforcement of traditional dependent trading relations
(b) an increase in the presence and power of foreign capital — particularly USA — in the local economy
(c) increased indebtedness
(d) increased technological and cultural dependence.

4. The Impact of the New Policies to Date

The impact of the shift in economic policy and reversal of the political direction of the government on the society has been profound and far-reaching. The national and international jubilation at the JLP victory has paled into cautious optimism (remember Rockefeller's warning!) and a creeping cynicism. The honeymoon is already over ; and we now seek to explain why.

(a) Impacts on Different Classes

For the working class, there has been unemployment and massive lay-offs, under the guise of reorganization, and the promise of "90,000" new jobs. Wherever there have been lay-offs in the State sector, the operational criterion has been party affiliation. Even the highest levels of the work force (managers and professionals) have been victimized. In fact these are the cases that come most readily to public attention, while the ordinary worker is dismissed with scarcely a whimper of protest. Wherever the lay-offs have been in the private sector, it is the union delegates — regardless of political affiliation — who are victimized first.

Workers have felt the unbridled arrogance of managers in their abrogation of contracts, in their intransigence in pay negotiations, and in arbitrary discipline and dismissals. The arrogance of the managerial classes derive from the political security and confidence they have that the government will support them. And right they are, for the JLP government itself is not averse to violation of the most fundamental industrial relations principles. The case brought by the NWU on behalf of JBC workers against the management is a prime example. The intransigence of the government and its unwillingness to negotiate with the junior doctors led to the virtual collapse of the public health system during the two week strike. Similarly the Jamaica Telephone Company was at an impasse with its operators for over six weeks.

There was widespread and militant industrial action in almost all sectors of the economy during the second three months of the new government. Those in the State sector were particularly serious. The government has sought to pin the industrial unrest on the communists, but this is futile. The simple fact is that some negotiations had been pending from before the election and, at any rate, workers' expectations had been raised by the promises of the JLP's campaign. In the haste to discover communist subversives behind every dispute, the government spokesmen smeared even its own loyal supporters. Such excesses always spawn the opposite result to what was intended.

By the summer of 1981, except for sporadic outbreaks, there was an uneasy industrial peace. The government imposed rather than negotiated a wage increase on the workers in the State sector. It could do this because of its political prestige and the threat of unemployment over the workers' heads.

For the small farmers, Deliverance has meant the curtailment of the land lease programme and several subsidies, all pending reorganization and/or investigation. But this is minor, compared to the loss of markets and the fall in the prices of local foodstuffs resulting from the massive importation of food.

The ganja farmers too are disappointed with Deliverance. Encouraged to plant ganja by certain party cadres, the farmers met increased pressure from the new government. Farms were burned, airstrips destroyed and dealers jailed. The industry is virtually in total collapse. Government's actions derive from some kind of understanding with the Reagan Administration to stop the export of ganja to the USA. The ganja industry is important to – and perhaps potentially the most dynamic component of – the peasant economy. Rural incomes from government programmes and from ganja and food crop production have fallen sharply.

The middle classes who remained in Jamaica find increasing competition from returning exiles for housing and for jobs (inevitably the ethnic contradictions surface). Thus living costs – housing, utilities, for example – have risen steeply. At the same time there is a flood of imported consumer goods which has eased the hardship of shortages.

Periodic shortages of essential goods — sugar, flour, soap powder — recur nevertheless.

For the capitalists, economic prospects are mixed. In the short-run business is bad ("the worst 8 months in years") as the domestic market has shrunk. There is still a severe shortage of foreign exchange as the promises of massive inflows of private investment are yet to materialize. IMF money is only sufficient to pay arrears on contracts and loans and to purchase basic imports.

Local manufacturers now face free competition from imports as a consequence of Deregulation. Prior to the election, imported substitutes sold on the black market were far more expensive. Both the manufacturers and the merchants are constrained by a shrinking domestic market, a consequence of the IMF Agreement.

In the vicious competition for markets, the first to be hurt were the higglers. They could no longer compete with the "big man and his trailer" of goods. Still they persist in the margins of the economy where scarcity appears or where there are not sufficient profits to attract the big merchant. But many small and medium manufacturers and shop-keepers have succumbed to the competition as well. All too often they have had to vacate rented facilities and shops at short notice. Many of the self-exiled owners are returning to reestablish their businesses, now that the political climate suits them.

The tyranny of the short run over the long run works against this government as well. In the long run the government promises there will be a buoyant economy kept afloat by massive waves of foreign investment. In the short-run only those who can export or hold on to a sufficient piece of the domestic market will survive.

For landlords, the demand for land and houses by exiles flush with US dollars has created a bonanza. Over the night of the election, real estate values doubled and more. They too are far more arrogant in their relations with tenants under the new government.

For the youth, the promises have already evaporated. Youth programmes have either been cut from the budget or held at nominal levels. With a slow start in the government's recovery programme, there are no jobs. Hustling scarce commodities and ganja now offer limited opportunities.

In July 1981, the Bank of Jamaica issued a gloomy report on the state of the economy. For the first six months, only bauxite had shown any growth among the major exports. It was known then by the Government that there would be at least a 10% drop in production during the last half of the year. Tourism, a major component in the government export production policy, had not started to turn around. Who could expect that so delicate an industry would so quickly shake off the bad image portrayed by the press for years, in the midst of a recession in North America?

The Bank reported that whereas exports were up by 20% over the same period of 1980, imports were up by 30%. Much of the increase was food to flood the market and eliminate the black market. This caused, as well, severe dislocation in agriculture as food crop and dairy farmers could not compete with foreign substitutes. The consumer price index rose only 0.7% from January to May 1981 as compared to 12.6% for the same period in 1980. This is, however, a curious statistic which has been challenged by consumer groups whose experience at the cash register suggests a higher rate of increase in the cost of living.

The report is issued monthly by the Bank of Jamaica's research department. For the first time, as far as we are aware, a qualifying statement was subsequently issued which tried to back track on some of the negative inferences of the report. This curious incident no doubt bruised the professional feelings of some of the Bank's staff.

(b) Impact on the Body Social/Body Politic

The coming to power of the JLP has sharply reversed certain democratic trends which were allowed to flower by the previous regime. The participation of workers in decision-making at the work place and, through their organizations, in national decisions has been severely curtailed. Above we pointed out that certain fundamental rights of workers have been flaunted by the government itself.

Appointees to government boards have been drawn largely from the propertied and middle classes. This is a sharp reversal of the broad social character of boards appointed by the previous government. Decision-making within the State itself has been centralized even more. The Prime Minister for example, has been criticized by columnists fiercely loyal to him, for wanting to make all the decisions and not delegating sufficient responsibility to his junior Ministers.

Access to the government owned radio and telvision by popular groupings and political opponents of the government has been sharply curtailed.

The political education programming has been replaced with imported (American) entertainment — sports, serials, pro-American films etc. The *Daily News* remains a forum for popular expression, but it, too, is to be sold. The government's problem is that only the *Daily News* workers want to buy it and they don't have enough money.

The anti-democratic character of the regime is evident in its political culture as well. It has resurrected the jacket-and-tie as official dress, as well as much of the trappings of old colonial Jamaica — the Governor General was knighted by the Queen (of England) and the Prime Minister became one of her Privy Councillors. One of the government's most loyal businesswoman supporters used a television news commentary slot to plead for a return to "our European" heritage and culture and a de-emphasis of the African. The Vice-Minister of Culture (Ed Bartlett) announced that all the cultures in Jamaica should be equally represented in national cultural programmes. These views are patently absurd in a country that is 98% African — including the mixed elements with which that Minister identifies himself. No minority is as large as 1% of the population. Evidently if the African culture is to be held in check or confined, it must mean that the majority of the people are to be dominated by an Anglo-American oriented culture.

Politically, despite all that was said, Jamaica was a free country under the PNP. So free that the JLP openly sabotaged and mobilized confrontations with government policy. At the other extreme, the communist movement was allowed to flourish. The new government is pledged to anti-communism. It is quick to discern communist conspiracies behind every industrial dispute and social protest. There are now calls from Cabinet Ministers for strong action against subversive elements. The intimidation and harassment of the WPJ and other left-wing elements has escalated sharply in recent months. The political stage is being set, it is believed, for a suppression of communism law.

All of the changes flow from the logic of the social and political character of the regime. It is the instrument of a degenerate ruling class that perceived real and imagined threats to their property, status and privilege from the PNP government and the democratic movement it led. They seek political vengeance against the progressives and communists and a quick rip-off of profits while the favourable political climate lasts. Under the PNP regime, the democratization of the State and the migration of the ethnic minorities brought more poor and middle income people into positions of social power and influence. Naturally, most of these people were black and brown. With the reversals, they are being replaced or shunted aside by brown and socially white people from the middle and propertied classes.

5. Whither the New Path

A generation of Caribbean scholars established their reputations criticising the policies of "industrialization by invitation". The historical experience of Jamaica in the 60's testify to the bankruptcy of these policies. In the text we have shown how the development path oriented around foreign investment in export production foundered on its own contradictions. While it brought growth, income was increasingly unequally distributed. Further it marginalized the mass of the population and restricted political rights and mass cultural expression.

International conditions were much more favourable for this kind of development policy in the 1960's. In the 70's and 80's the USA has become more protectionist. The crisis of the 70's has brought restrictive monetary policy and high interest rates to the USA and the UK. It is precisely the unfavourable climate for international investment that underpins Rockefeller's caution against undue expectations of foreign inflows.

Further the price of foreign investment to the society will be high. If an investor can get 20% on his money at a US bank, at what rate of profit must he exploit the Jamaican worker to make it worth his while? Investors are attracted not only by cheap wages, but by a disciplined labour force. And the record of the Jamaican working class is poor in this respect.

The two pillars upon which the success of the government's policy will depend are foreign investment and internal repression. Over the former, it has no control. The less foreign investment the more necessary will be internal repression to contain the social contradictions and frustrations. And a greater flow of foreign investment can only materialize by putting the trade unions under heavy manners.

6. The Resistance

Finally, we turn to the opposition to the government's policies. In the election, the PNP polled 349,000 votes and the JLP 501,000. There is therefore a sizeable hard-core of support for the PNP policies of Democratic Socialism which withstood the lures and pressures of the JLP campaign. But this large minority has had very little leadership since the election.

The PNP has been kept disorganized ostensibly by a leadership crisis. At the base is an apparently irreconcilable conflict between the two wings of the party. Whereas the personality of Manley transcended these divisions and galvanized a nationalist unity in the past, the sharpness of the class struggle in the '70's makes this impossible in the 80's. Nevertheless, this personality remains the dominant one among the progressive forces. Manley has deliberately remained quiet, partly to allow the JLP to get mired in the real problems they scoffed at while in opposition. The other reason for his silence is to keep the party immobilized until he can sort out his own plans and a strategy for resolving the internal conflict. It is widely known that he is hostile to the left, as he regards the communist affiliations as the principal cause of the defeat.

The WPJ has been under pressure from the eve of the election when elements of the security forces and judiciary loyal to the JLP began to sense a victory for their party. Since the election these cadres have been victimized and subjected to continuous harassment, the latest being an attempt to link the leadership to terrorism. Despite the pressures they have stood up well and have provided what little national leadership there has been for the socialist opposition. It is likely that they will be the chief scapegoats for the government as resistance develops to the new order.

It is too early to speculate on how the class/race contradictions will manifest themselves. That they will, history assures us. In the 70's these struggles became so sharp that the brown middle class abandoned the leadership of the national movement it had arrogated unto itself in 1938. They had held responsibility for only one generation of Jamaicans (1962-1980). Unable to employ, feed, shelter, educate and promote their well-being they abandoned the historical tasks to the socially white capitalist ruling class.

The next time the masses of people rise, they will have to lead themselves.

APPENDIX

THE IMF, DEMOCRATIC SOCIALISM AND ZIG-ZAG POLITICS: JAMAICA, 1976-1977

The Present as History

The massive defeat of Michael Manley's Peoples National Party (PNP) in the October 30, 1980 electoral contest was a logical result of a process that began on or before December 15, 1976. In the book Small Garden, Bitter Weed, for which these two documents are an Appendix, we describe and analyse the struggle against imperialism, led by Manley's PNP government between 1974 and 1979, and the reaction of imperialism to that struggle (cf. Chapter 8).

The most crucial year of that period was September 1976 to September 1977. It was in September 1976 that Manley and the Jamaican people declared unequivocally that WE ARE NOT FOR SALE. WE KNOW WHERE WE ARE GOING, at a mass meeting in the National Stadium. Unknown to the Jamaican people, the then Minister of Finance (David Coore) and senior officials of the Bank of Jamaica (Governor Arthur Brown and Co.) were busy at that very moment negotiating with the International Monetary Fund (IMF) to "sell" Jamaica by ensnaring the economy deeper in the net of imperialism. The Finance Minister had made a firm commitment to the Fund at a September meeting in Manila, Philippines. And between September and December 1976, Bank of Jamaica officials held secret meetings with IMF officials deliberately "disguised as tourists" on the north coast of Jamaica.

Meanwhile the PNP launched a militant anti-imperialist electoral campaign that presented "Democratic Socialism" to the Jamaican people as the answer to centuries of exploitation under colonialism and imperialism. The opposing Jamaica Labour Party (JLP) offered what they called "Nationalism" ; in reality, Jamaican capitalism in association with imperialism.

In the election held on December 15, 1976 the electorate gave Manley and the PNP an overwhelming mandate to pursue the Democratic Socialist alternative. Right after this electoral outcome a small group of political economists from the University of the West Indies alerted the General Secretary of the PNP (Dr. D. K. Duncan) and Prime Minister

Manley of the consequences of an IMF agreement and the 40% devaluation of the currency which that entailed.

Prime Minister Manley commissioned us to prepare an alternative to the IMF, in the spirit of the electoral mandate. The first document reproduced here was submitted to him late December 1976; and discussions arising from it led to a declaration made by him in a national broadcast on January 5, 1977 that his government would reject the IMF solution and chart the nation on a "self-reliant democratic socialist" path. This position was re-emphasised and elaborated in a second broadcast on January 19, 1977 by which time the UWI political economists had elaborated the Democratic Socialist alternative in two other documents.

The Prime Minister's speech of January 19 promised the nation that an Emergency Production Plan would be formulated by March to guide government policy and action for the rest of 1977 and that by year-end a Five-Year Development Plan would be ready for public scrutiny. To facilitate this, he invited members of the UWI team to take up key positions in the state planning, policy and mobilization bureaucracy. The most important of these appointments were Dr. N.P. Girvan to be Chief Technical Director of the National Planning Agency with Dr. M. Witter as his Economic Adviser; and Mr. L.G. Lindsay as Chief Technical Director in the newly-created Ministry of National Mobilization and Human Resource Development.

The National Planning Agency (NPA) organized a Task Force of state and University technocrats, trade union representatives, and other interest groups while the Ministry of Mobilization invited suggestions from the Jamaican public. Over 10,000 responses were received from the public in a two-week period. And these were integrated into a massive three-volume plan[1] submitted by the NPA to cabinet on March 23, 1977. That plan was subsequently rejected by government. For a month later, on April 22, 1977, Prime Minister Manley presented to Parliament an *Emergency Production Plan, 1977-78* (summarized by API as *The Peoples Plan*) that involved capitulation to the IMF and imperialism.

The mandate of December 15, 1976 was betrayed there and then. What happened thereafter closely parallels the analysis provided in Document No. 1. The IMF and imperialism finally succeeded in removing the Manley government on October 30, 1980.

As indicated in that document, part of the price Mr. Manley would have to pay to receive IMF assistance would be to put the left wing of his party "under heavy manners". The first IMF agreement was signed in July 1977; and at the annual party conference in September, Manley took to himself tasks, in both party and state, that had been the main responsibility of the leader of the left wing — Dr. D.K. Duncan; thereby forcing Duncan's resignation from his dual role as General Secretary of the PNP and Minister of National Mobilization and Human Resource Development.

Soon after this Michael Witter wrote Document No. 2 for self clarification and for discussion among the UWI Team as to whether or not we should continue to work with the regime. That document provides an incisive analysis of the 9-month period following the December 15, 1976 electoral mandate for Democratic Socialism. It exposes the contradictions inherent in the betrayal of the mandate and the analysis provided a great deal of foresight of events which subsequently materialized.

Eventually, more information and documentation will become available to provide us with much more in-depth analyses of the critical conjuncture that existed in Jamaica in the four months between December 1976 and April 1977. Most of this is perhaps only now available to the one individual, Mr. Michael Manley, who took the critical decision to keep Jamaica handcuffed to imperialism. In the book itself, we have offered a very brief and unsatisfactory analysis of "what factors triggered the turn-back of Prime Minister Manley ...." (p. 93). One thing is certain . history will never absolve him!

November 16, 1980   George L. Beckford

---

[1] Volume I, described as "The Peoples Plan", provided a synthesis of the overall "Emergency Production Plan" ; Volume II consisted of detailed sector-by-sector plans; and Volume III, called "The Voice of the People", reproduced in abridged form the 10,000 suggestions made by the public.

THE ZIGS AND ZAGS OF THE GREAT DEMOCRATIC SOCIALIST EVOLUTION

The Spring of Hope

Despite the many who would try to forget, the people of Jamaica voted a massive mandate for Democratic Socialism on December 15, 1976. The election in fact occurred at a historical conjuncture characterized by :

(i) an intensive political struggle between the forces of imperialism and the progressive anti-imperialist forces ; and

(ii) a severe economic crisis which was principally manifested in projected budgetary and balance of payment deficits.

Any sensible analysis of the nature and causes of the economic crisis must ultimately be rooted in the domination of the economy by imperialism, particularly North American imperialism. We must not forget that it was the foreign-owned bauxite and alumina companies which had cut-back production in 1975, partly as a result of a slump in the economy of the U.S.A., partly to discipline Jamaican workers and partly to discipline the PNP regime for imposing the Production Levy. It was the foreign-owned and dominated banking sector which facilitated the flight of local capital in proportions hitherto unknown in Jamaica (about $300 million in 1976 alone), while restricting credit and calling in loans to local businessmen. Often on the advice of these banks, foreign capitalists decided to forego investment opportunities in what was perceived as a hostile political climate. Similarly much of the blame for the decline in tourism must rest with the foreign press which waged an adverse publicity campaign against Jamaica on the basis of distorted and exaggerated reports submitted by its local reactionary agents. Finally, the worldwide crisis of imperialism meant weak commodity prices for traditional exports, sugar and banana, on which Jamaica depended for foreign exchange.

All of this constituted the economic content of a policy of destabilization waged by the imperialists and its local reactionary agents against the previous PNP government. The economic squeeze along with the flight of local capital and sabotage by big Jamaican capitalists accounted for the foreign exchange and budgetary crisis with which the government is now grappling. In reality, while the progressive forces were scoring a political victory over the forces of imperialism on December 15, 1976, the imperialists were scoring far more significant victories on the economic front by crippling the Jamaican economy.

In the context of the PNP's campaign platform and the people's mandate in response to the threat of imperialism, the newly elected government correctly chose to solve the economic crisis with methods which would .

(i) weaken the imperialist control of the economy in the long run;
(ii) halt the deterioration in the standard of living of the broad masses who had rallied to the support of the government; and
(iii) continue the programme of social and economic reforms.

It was in the spirit of broad democratic and progressive support for the anti-imperialist PNP government, that the UWI political economists approached the political directorate with a "Democratic Socialist Alternative" to the economic proposals of the IMF.

It is now well known, on account of leaks to the *Gleaner*, that in January 1977, there ensued a bitter struggle between the political economists and the incumbent rightwing technocrats under the political leadership of the Minister of Finance, who were advancing the conventional wisdom of IMF orthodoxy. The impact of this struggle has been to exacerbate the intra-cabinet tensions which continue to manifest themselves more and more openly. This is so despite the P.M.'s explicit statements in Parliament and NEC that the political economists were brought in by him and not Dr. Duncan.

In January, the P.M. made two historic speeches which raised the expectations of the broad masses, while driving fear into the hearts of foreign and local reactionaries. He announced that the government would in fact institute a programme of economic reform and not allow the economy to fall further into the clutches of imperialism. Such a programme of economic reform sought to minimize the burden of adjustment to the crisis which would fall on the shoulders

of the masses. The substantive content of the speeches of the 5th and 19th January were
- (i) identification of the IMF as the central banking institution of the imperialist system;
- (ii) rejection of the existing IMF conditions for balance of payments support. These were :
    - (a) massive devaluation — approximately 40% — of the currency;
    - (b) massive budget cuts;
    - (c) wages and incomes policy;
    - (d) unspoken conditions which would put the progressive forces under manners and make the climate hospitable to foreign capital.
- (iii) a fiscal programme which minimized the burden of taxes on the broad masses;
- (iv) a foreign exchange programme restricting unnecessary luxury expenditure and a carefully prepared budget for essential imports;
- (v) a call to the nation to engage in the battle for increased production and self-reliance under the guidance of an Emergency Production Plan to be presented in April; and
- (vi) a pledge to present a 5-year plan to guide the transition to socialism.

The process of planning was entrusted to the leadership of the UWI political economists who took up, on the invitation of the P.M. (January 20, 1977) senior positions within the bureaucracy on February 1, 1977. Acting within the terms of reference laid down by the political directorate, the people as a whole and large sections of the bureaucracy were mobilized to draft an Emergency Production Plan for :
- (i) increasing national production to fill the short-fall of imports due to limited foreign exchange; as a matter of priority, to increase the production of food, clothing and shelter;
- (ii) increased employment, at best; at worst, halt further unemployment. This would, of course assume, in the context of the January 19 speech that the Emergency Production Plan would begin:
    - (a) to lay the basis for a self-reliant economy;

(b) further the democratization of the economy, particularly at the point of production; and
(c) develop relations with the socialist world in order to reduce the stranglehold of imperialism.

All of this promised a spring of hope for the progressive, anti-imperialist forces in the nation, a hope which progressively waned under the unchecked onslaught of the forces of reaction. Smarting from the political defeat of December 15 and the apparent economic defeat of January 19, the reactionaries regrouped and began a vicious counter-attack. The *Gleaner* became more strident in promoting rumours of left-wing plots and in orchestrating a virtual blackmail by local capitalists : they held the production of the country in ransom for economic policy which favoured their interests. Divisiveness among the progressive forces provided the openings for increased pressure on the left, inside and outside the party. It was during this period that it became clear that contrary to popular perception, the IMF had not been defeated in January. Instead the political and economic bases for concluding an agreement with the IMF were being quietly laid. On April 22, the P.M. announced an IMF package which was substantially inconsistent with the draft EPP − The People's Plan − which had been presented to the Political Directorate on March 23.

The Long Hot Summer

The principal impact of April 22 was to spread confusion in the minds of the masses as to the direction the government had really chosen. Workers who had accepted a voluntary wage restraint since Jamuary and peasants who had awaited a signal from the government on the land question, began to wonder whether this was not in fact a capitalist plan. While there was some criticism by the extra-PNP left − particularly the WLL − in the immediate post-April 22 period, the progressive forces adopted a wait-and-see attitude. They argued that even valid criticism would further weaken the beleaguered government and that their role should be to see to the implementation of whatever marginal socialist policy there was.

The local reactionaries on the other hand intensified their attacks, particularly in the *Gleaner,* against the left and went as far as to propose a military solution to the political deadlock within the PNP. Out of the crevices in whch they had sought refuge after December 15, crawled reactionary spokesmen to sing the praises of capitalism and denounce socialism. Rumours of conspiracy within the PNP and between the PNP left and the Marxist left gained renewed currency.

The JLP seized the opportunity to develop a range of front organizations, particularly the WFM, JAH and a farmers' organization. In a fashion, frighteningly analogous to the response of the Chilean reactionaries, they mounted nationwide demonstrations over shortages of essential consumer goods, unemployment and generally severe hardship of the masses.

The government sent its emissaries, Patterson and Coore, to the imperialists; in return they sent theirs — Young and Rosalyn Carter. The result was a mutual pronouncement of improved relations between the Manley and Carter regimes. In addition, the P.M. held talks with Trudeau and Callaghan at the Commonwealth Conference in London. It is clear that these exchanges facilitated a positive response from the IMF to Jamaica's proposals in request of foreign loans. The price of this renewed friendship must have included a down-playing of anti-imperialist rhetoric and the political education it would necessarily entail.

After much foot-dragging by elements of the government, a successful mission was also sent to the USSR, out of which came an exchange of ambassadors and potential long-term economic and cultural agreements. Whether or not sufficient follow-up work to conclude these negotiations successfully is being done in the appropriate agencies is an open question.

In June the government concluded a two-year agreement with the IMF which was not substantially different from traditional IMF agreements. Instead of a unitary devaluation, a temporary two-tiered system, converging ultimately to a devalued single exchange rate, was introduced, largely as political cosmetics. In every other respect, the agreement was the same as was expected : a severe wages and income policy, drastic budget cuts, removal of import restrictions, conditions on new loans, etc.

By the end of the 'long hot summer', the WLL was forced to mount mass manifestations.
 (i) against local big capitalists who were holding consumers and workers to ransom;
 (ii) against elements of the political directorate who were agitating for and formulating economic policy in the interests of big capitalists and against the masses;
 (iii) in support of workers' control of *Daily News* as a structural response to the ultra-reactionary *Gleaner;* and
 (iv) in support of the government against the new tactics of imperialism: a hollow friendly posture, and a hypocritical call for Human Rights.

In addition, the consciousness of the masses, heightened by the anti-imperialist struggle, has made them quickly appreciate the significance of the Chilean experience to the contemporary Jamaican situation. This widespread understanding among progressive people caused them to view with alarm:
 (a) the *Gleaner* in its role as *El Mercurio,* spouting anti-communist venom, and anti-government propaganda and singing the praises of capitalism and imperialism;
 (b) housewives, organized by reactionaries, demonstrating over shortages and the deteriorating standard of living;
 (c) shortages of the same consumer goods as in Chile soap, butter, detergent, tea, etc.;
 (d) economic strangulation by the imperialists; and
 (e) continued economic sabotage by local capitalists.

And they began to wonder whether the military would not in fact respond to the call of the Hearnes and Perkins!

In Autumn, They Say the Leaves Fall

As we have indicated above, the IMF agreement was inconsistent with the People's Plan and objectively imposed severe constraints on the possibilities of socialist transformation. Prices began to rise sharply as a result of the devaluation. Together with the imposed wages policy, a dearth of jobs, and shortages of essential goods, the working class was angered and began to express this through intensified industrial disputes. The IMF imposed budget cuts in August signalled further unemployment and undermined the political and financial bases for implementing a meaningful 5-year plan.

Mounting social manifestations by the reactionaries and counter-manifestations by progressive forces under the leadership of the WLL, prompted a response from the PNP. The response had to be contradictory. On the one hand, it had to assure the masses that the government had not succumbed to the pressure of the imperialists and its local reactionary agents (the Big Man). On the other hand, it had to assure the capitalists that it would control and silence the demands of the progressive elements within the PNP. These elements had in fact not engaged in any public attacks on the reactionaries since late Spring. But as part of its campaign to accuse the left of imaginary conspiracies, and to cast them as scapegoats for the non-performance of the so-called private sector, the reactionaries had seized on every utterance of the left, particularly those of the Minister of Mobilization and the PNP Y.O., wrenched them out of their respective contexts and used them to condemn the political directorate for permitting so-called "divisive rhetoric". In such a climate, the capitalists and their imperialist bosses argued, there could be no increased production and foreign loans would be hard to raise because capitalists had no confidence in the government.

The PNP mounted a mass demonstration in support of its own government and the Prime Minister addressed a mass rally at the end of the march. He pronounced united support for the leftist and the rightist elements of the Cabinet who were under public attack, announced the acquisition of RJR and Seprod(?), and promised a clear definition of PNP policy at the annual party conference on September 5 to 8. At the conference, the intra-party tensions, reflecting as they must the tensions in the wider society, heightened and forced the cancellation of the vice-presidential elections. In the public session, the Prime Minister pledged his party to increasing production and assumed control over the Land Reform Unit from the Ministry of Mobilization and the Party from the General Secretary. It meant a significant down-grading of Dr. Duncan and by implication the PNP left had been put under manners.

Dr. Duncan has been the first leaf to fall this Autumn. He resigned both posts on September 15 on the grounds that the loss of confidence in him by the Party resulting from hostile physical attacks and rumour-mongering by party rightists, made him incapable of performing his job. Before speculating as to whether other "leaves" (leftist) will fall or not, it is best to pause and re-examine the shifting class alliances and objective economic constraints on government policy.

The election was won with the support of large sections of the peasantry, most of the working class, progressive and patriotic elements within the middle-classes and the petit bourgeois as a whole. To be sure there was a sprinkling of support from patriotic elements within the bourgeoisie, but overall leadership was vested in progressive petit bourgeois elements. On the side of reaction, there was also a multi-class alliance, but it was headed by the reactionary ruling class of big capitalistists — particularly the merchants and landlords. By the time summer 1977 came around, it was evident that middle class and big bourgeois supporters of the PNP had defected to reaction. Most important were the signs that petit bourgeois support for the PNP was being eroded. With economic conditions worsening throughout the year, and very little new employment in sight, there is every reason to believe that working class support for the PNP will diminish. Similarly, unless the government can meet the expectations of the land hungry peasantry, it will be faced with land capturing on a massive scale.

The logic of the shifting class alliances must be understood within the context of the objective constraints on government policy imposed largely by the IMF agreement. The agreement severely restricted the size of the government's budget and established a tight ceiling on the amount of both foreign and local loans. There is very little "pork in the barrel" to satisfy the demands for jobs and land. Prices will continue to rise until the unitary devalued exchange rate is reached in early 1978. With a vigilantly enforced wages and incomes policy which will allow not much more than a $10 per week increase in pay, workers' productivity is bound to fall on account of partial or total withdrawal of their efforts, resulting from low motivation and more frequent industrial disputes.

It is hoped that the IMF agreement would trigger $200 million worth of foreign loans to meet the requirements of the economy, particularly raw materials for manufacturing. At the end of September, only about a half of this had materialized. There was clear evidence that the government, despite having agreed to the IMF's conditions, were being strung out by the imperialists who wanted even further concessions.

Even if the loans are raised, there is no reason to assume production will automatically be significantly boosted. In normal years, capitalists have used import licences to ship money out of the country; in uncertain times such as these, they cannot be expected to desist from this practice. They refuse to invest in expanded production on the grounds that they have no confidence in a regime which harbours socialists and communists.

It is obvious that the further concession which the IMF and other foreign capitalists, as well as local big capitalists, want is that the left inside and outside of the PNP be put under manners. As a result of financial blackmail by foreign capitalists and investment blackmail by local capitalists, there apparently have been realignments of power within the Political Directorate, with the left suffering serious losses. As a part of the same process, there is also a process of realignment of power within the bureaucracy, again with the isolation and weakening of the left. The struggle at the National Housing Trust, the downgrading of the Ministry of National Mobilization and the increasing marginalization of the National Planning Agency bear witness to this.

Such an analysis suggests that foreign loans and the confidence of the bourgeoisie can only be bought at the expense of the left within the party and the progressive movement as a whole. Despite the subjective desires of the political directorate, it cannot now alter that path it has now chosen and must purge the party, the government and the bureaucracy of all control by the left. One would therefore expect that D.K. is only the first of many leftist leaves to fall. Political technology might dictate the purging of overtly treacherous or politically insignificant rightists. Whether or not this will serve as a sufficient cosmetic for the left to be purged, without the government's mass support deserting, remains to be seen.

The Winter of Discontent

We have argued that the government has locked itself onto a specific path as a result of the IMF agreement. The alternative path projected in March by the EPP is no longer feasible. That path required a type of national mobilization which would have called not only for anti-imperialist and socialist rhetoric but for substantial changes in income distribution and economic re-structuring. Such a mobilization and income redistribution would further antagonize capital and cannot be tolerated under the present circumstances. At best the government can try to re-negotiate certain of the conditions. Even if the IMF responds favourably, the straitjacket it has imposed on government policy will be essentially the same. It will not be easy to cosmetize further devaluations. In October, despite the success which will be claimed of the re-negotiations, a further depreciation of the currency, with all its consequences, is on the agenda.

It is rather imperative that the government devise a strategy for reducing expectations, as the Americans suggested during their visit. The logic of the economic path chosen is such as to reveal more and more the government's rightist tendencies. The more of the left it sheds, the more credibility it will lose among the masses. Nor will it regain sufficient credibility among the bourgeoise to earn its loyalty. Increasingly it will have to utilize State power to repress mass demonstrations whether organized by the left or the reactionary JLP. At this juncture, the left for a variety of historically specific reasons, must receive the principal wrath of the State. The *Gleaner* is already laying the basis for a resurgence of anti-communism with a spate of attacks on Marxism and Communism. Anti-communist sentiment is just beneath the skin of large sections of the masses — workers, peasants, petit bourgeois, etc. All that is needed for its release is a signal from the political directorate, a signal which will result from the logic of the present process of political realignments within the PNP, if it is not firmly checked.

How much discontent this winter will bring turns on the following:

(a) whether the unions can hold workers to the wage guidelines;
(b) whether the extra-PNP left will agitate against the deteriorating economic conditions of the masses;
(c) whether the land hungry peasants are prepared to wait until the constitution is changed;
(d) whether sufficient consumer goods can be imported to bribe the middle classes;
(e) whether the JLP will step up their harassment of the government;
(f) whether the forces of reaction will rest until the entire left is purged from the PNP and suppressed, along with the communists, thereafter;
(g) whether the lumpen proletariat will intensify its predatory violence; and
(h) whether the loyalty of the security forces to the government is greater than that of the Chilean army to Allende.

All of these questions will of course soon be answered in a fashion for which no one, least of all the progressive forces, will be prepared.

Michael Witter
September 30, 1977

BIBLIOGRAPHY

SUGGESTED FURTHER READINGS

This list of references is provided for the stimulated reader to probe deeper into the issues posed in this book. It is by no means an exhaustive bibliography.

CHAPTER 1

CORNFORTH, Maurice, *Materialism and the Dialectical Method*, International Publishers, N.Y., 1972.

CORNFORTH, Maurice, *Historical Materialism*, International Publishers, N.Y., 1972.

CORNFORTH, Maurice, *The Theory of Knowledge*, International Publishers, N.Y., 1972.

(These three works are volumes in a collection called *Dialectical Materialism: An Introduction*, by Maurice Cornforth, International Publishers, N.Y.)

EATON, John, *Political Economy*, International Publishers, N.Y., 1975.

LANGE, O., *Political Economy*, Vol. I, II, Pergamon Press, N.Y., 1971.

LEONTYEV, A., *Political Economy*, Progress Publishers, 1974.

POLITZER, Georges, *Elementary Principles of Philosophy*, International Publishers, N.Y., 1976.

TSE-TUNG, Mao, "On Contradiction" in *Four Essays on Philosophy*, Foreign Languages Press, Peking, 1968.

CHAPTERS 2 and 3

BRATHWAITE, E. Kamau, *Caribbean Man in Space and Time*, Savacou Publications, Mona, 1974.

BRATHWAITE, E. Kamau, *The Arrivants – A Trilogy*, OUP, 1973.

BRATHWAITE, E. Kamau, *Contradictory Omens*, Savacou Publications, Mona, 1974.

FANON, F., *The Wretched of the Earth*, Penguin Books, Harmondsworth, 1967.

HUBERMAN, L., *Man's Worldly Goods*, Monthly Review Press, New York and London, 1968.

JAMES, C.L.R., *Black Jacobins*, N.Y., Vintage Books, 1963.

LENIN, V.I., *Imperialism: The Highest Stage of Capitalism*, Progress Publishers, Moscow; also Peking Foreign Languages Press, 1970.

MARX, K. and ENGELS, F., *The Communist Manifesto*, Peking Foreign Languages Press, 1975.

MEMMI, A., *The Colonizer and the Colonized*, Beacon Press, Boston, 1970.

RODNEY, W., *How Europe Underdeveloped Africa*, Bogle-L'Ouverture Publications, London and Tanzania Publishing House, Dar-es-Salaam, 1972.

WILLIAMS, E., *Capitalism and Slavery*, Second Edition, London: Andre Deutsch, 1964.

CHAPTERS 4 and 5

BECKFORD, George, *Persistent Poverty*, Oxford University Press, N.Y., I.S.E.R., Kingston, 1972.

BRATHWAITE, Edward, *The Development of Creole Society in Jamaica*, Clarendon Press, London, 1972.

BRATHWAITE, E. Kamau, *Caribbean Man in Space and Time*, Savacou Publications, Mona. 1974.

EISNER, Gisela, *Jamaica 1830–1930: A Study in Economic Growth*, Manchester University Press, Manchester, 1961.

HALL, Douglas, *Free Jamaica, 1838–1865*, Caribbean Universities Press, 1969.

JACQUES-GARVEY, A., *Philosophy and Opinions of Marcus Garvey*, Atheneum, New York, 1977.

LEWIS, Arthur W., *The Evolution of the Peasantry in the British West Indies*, Colonial Office Pamphlet 656, 1936.

MARSHALL, Woodville K., "Notes on Peasant Development in the West Indies since 1838", *Social and Economic Studies*, Vol. 17, No. 3, U.W.I., I.S.E.R., Sept. 1968.

MUNROE, T. and ROBOTHAM, D., *Struggles of the Jamaican People*, Workers' Liberation League, Kingston, 1977.

CHAPTERS 6 and 7

BECKFORD, George (Ed.), *Caribbean Economy*, U.W.I., I.S.E.R., 1975.

CARNEGIE, James, *Some Aspects of Jamaican Politics 1918-1938*, Institute of Jamaica, Kingston, 1973.

GIRVAN, Norman, *Foreign Capital and Economic Underdevelopment in Jamaica*, U.W.I., I.S.E.R., 1972.

GIRVAN, Norman and JEFFERSON, Owen, *Readings in the Political Economy of the Caribbean*, New World Publishers, 1971.

GIRVAN, Norman, *Corporate Imperialism, Conflict and Expropriation*, Monthly Review Press, 1979.

JEFFERSON, Owen C. *The Post-War Economic Development of Jamaica*, U.W.I., I.S.E.R., 1972.

MUNROE, T. and LEWIS, R., *Readings in Government and Politics of the West Indies*, U.W.I., Department of Government, 1969.

MUNROE, T., *The Politics of Constitutional Decolonisation in Jamaica, 1944–1962*, U.W.I., I.S.E.R., 1972.

POST, Ken, *Arise Ye Starvelings: The Jamaican Labour Rebellion of 1938 and its Aftermath*, Martinus Nijhoff, The Hague/Boston/London, 1978.

STONE, Carl, *Electoral Behaviour and Public Opinion in Jamaica*, U.W.I., I.S.E.R., 1973.

STONE, Carl, *Race, Class and Politics in Urban Jamaica*, U.W.I., I.S.E.R., 1974.

CHAPTER 8

MANLEY, M., *The Politics of Change*, Andre Deutsch, 1972.

MANLEY, M. and the Jamaican People, *Not For Sale*, Editorial Consultants Inc., San Francisco, U.S.A., 1977.

NATIONAL PLANNING AGENCY, *The People's Plan* (3 Vols.), EPP, 1977 ("Confidential" to Government of Jamaica, March 1977).

PEOPLE'S NATIONAL PARTY, *Principles and Objectives*, 1979.

STONE, C. and BROWN, Aggrey, *Essays on Power and Change*, Jamaica Publishing House, 1976.

CHAPTERS 9 and 10

GIRVAN, N., BERNAL, B, and HUGHES, W., "The IMF and the Third World: The Case of Jamaica, 1974-80", *Development Dialogue* (1980:2).

GOVERNMENT OF JAMAICA, *Five Year Development Plan, 1978-82: Main Document* (National Planning Agency, Kingston, 1978).

THOMAS, C.Y., *Dependence and Transformation: The Economics of the Transition to Socialism* (Monthly Review Press, New York, 1974).

WORLD BANK, *World Development Report 1978* (Oxford Univ. Press, New York, 1978).

WORLD BANK, *World Development Report 1979* (Oxford Univ. Press, New York, 1979).